Laughable Laws
and
Courtroom Capers

Laughable Laws and Courtroom Capers

Loony Legalities and Curious Cases
All Around the U.S.A.

Robert Wayne Pelton
author of *Loony Laws*
and
Loony Sex Laws

WALKER AND COMPANY ✹ NEW YORK

DEDICATED
TO
THE LEGISLATORS OF VIRGINIA
WHO ONCE WROTE AND THEN PASSED A STATUTE
TITLED: "TO PROHIBIT CORRUPT PRACTICES OR
BRIBERY BY ANY PERSON OTHER THAN
CANDIDATES."

First published in the United States of America in 1993
by Walker Publishing Company, Inc.

Published simultaneously in Canada by Thomas Allen & Son
Canada, Limited, Markham, Ontario

Library of Congress Cataloging-in-Publication Data
Pelton, Robert W., 1934–
Laughable laws and courtroom capers : loony legalities and
curious cases all around the U.S.A. / Robert Wayne Pelton.
p.   cm.
Includes index.
ISBN 0-8027-7390-7 (pbk.)
1. Law—United States—States—Humor.   2. Trials—United
States—States—Humor.   I. Title.
K184.P45   1993
349.73'0207—dc20
[347.300207]   92-20550
CIP

Printed in the United States of America

2   4   6   8   10   9   7   5   3   1

Contents

Part III
Courtroom Capers

vi

Preface

"My aim is not to pass laws, but to repeal them."
—Senator Barry Goldwater, 1961

Where do laws come from? There are four major sources of all laws. *Constitutional law* is simply law derived from the Constitution of the United States and the constitution of each state. Then there is what is known as *statutory law*. Next there is *regulatory law*. And last there's *common law*, the bedrock of English and American legal tradition.

Congressmen in Washington pass an ungodly maze of new federal laws each year. Politicians who fill the legislatures of every state swamp their constituents with a multitude of new laws annually. Such legislative gems are best known as statutes. Akin to state and federal statutes are regulations, or regulatory laws. Thousands of regulatory laws are written and issued as needed by various government bureaucrats who have been empowered by Congress to do so.

As new statutes are passed, courts at every level run a never-ending treadmill where opinion after opinion is handed down. Each new court case results in a new case law, better known as common law. Common law is no more than a judge's ruling. The following decision handed down by a New York City court in 1915 is a prime example. The judge declared: "It is disorderly conduct for one man to greet another man on the street by placing the end of his thumb against the tip of his nose, at the same time extending and wriggling the fingers of his hand." To say the least, such judge-made laws are often patently illegal and of questionable constitutionality.

Law is constantly changing. Politicians at every level of government—federal, state, county, city, community—chaotically pass an endless flood of new laws. There are so many that no one appears to know how to begin unraveling the horrid mess. Americans are deluged with new laws, while seldom does anyone bother rescinding any of the old ones.

Every state, every city, every county, and every community has its share of legal dinosaurs buried in the musty archives. Strange laws are often merely a reflection of the morals and attitudes of the time, or were written to deal with situations or social issues that are no longer relevant today. An example is an Illinois statute passed quite some time before the advent of the feminist movement. Politicians wrote this silly piece of legislation, which specified that all bachelors should henceforth be called Master instead of Mister when addressed by a female. Women would then unquestionably know the matrimonial score.

Ohio legislators once passed an odd law regarding politicians. The legislation prohibited their citizenry from not listening to any long-winded politician's speech on Memorial Day by playing croquet within one mile of the speaker's stand. The penalty for ignoring a boring orator was a $25 fine!

Some practical-joking lawmaker no doubt slipped the above legislation through by running it with a stack of others. He probably wanted to see if his fellow legislators actually paid attention to all of the various new laws before voting on them. Evidently they didn't.

Chief Justice Charles Evans Hughes aptly described how he felt regarding the passing of laws in America. He declared: "The United States is the greatest law factory the world has ever known." How do you feel about the Chief Justice's statement? Do you concur? Decide for yourself after carefully perusing the following bits of ludicrous legislation. Let's take a quick sojourn into the never-never land of ludicrous, laughable legalese before responding to this question.

I

LAUGHABLE LAWS

1

Introducing Ludicrous, Laughable Laws

If you sing at a bar in Wisconsin, own a shaving brush in Wagner, South Dakota, mispronounce the name Arkansas, marry your mother-in-law in Washington, D.C., or plant a poplar tree in New York City, you most certainly will run afoul of the law!

Peculiar, absurd, preposterous, and even weird are some of the legislative oddities, often still in force, to be found buried between the crumbling covers of America's obsolete statute books. Such legal fossils can be readily uncovered in every state of the Union, as well as in every county, city, and town. How silly it is when a law has to be passed telling farmers it's okay to sleep with their hogs! Imagine, if you will, that someone once deemed it necessary to pass a law prohibiting people from scaring a baby or impersonating Santa Claus.

So many laws have been passed over the years that nobody could possibly know what they all are. Laws simply pile up, year after year, burying each other and smothering the citizenry. Nothing, it appears, is beyond the reach of those who, once in public office, take it upon themselves to burden their fellow citizens with more and more and more silly laws—often laws that never should have been passed in the first place and, if contested, would certainly be thrown out of court.

Congress considers an average of 15,000 new federal laws each session. Of these, more than 500 are passed into law. During the same period, an average 250,000 bills are introduced in state legislatures throughout America; more than 50,000 become laws. Consequently, every person in the United States has an ungodly number of new laws to live by each year. And these figures don't even take into consideration the thousands of ordinances passed annually by various cities, counties, and towns. Exactly how much protection does the average American need?

Digging into the archives and old statute books will reveal an astounding number of unrepealed legislative oddities. According to an antiquated law in Sugartown, Louisiana, for example, it's against the law for politicians to "squirt tobacco juice" on a sidewalk while campaigning for public office. People in Tennessee who have dogs and cats "can't run at large." And

4

residents of Helena, Montana, are banned from unrestrained giggling while walking on city streets.

Some old laws, when uncovered, can be put to positive use. Here's an example of how one particular attorney, appointed by the court, defended a South Carolina man accused of shooting and killing a plain-clothes police officer. The fellow claimed that since the other man wasn't in uniform, he didn't know his identity. Mistaking him for a burglar, he pulled out his own pistol and fired.

The story was plausible, but the defense attorney couldn't explain why his client was carrying a gun in the first place. Searching through South Carolina archives he found a statute, dating back to Colonial times, which made it unlawful to attend church on Sunday without carrying a weapon. By maneuvers based on this legal holdover, the attorney was able to convince the judge and jury to the extent that the fellow was able to get off with a verdict of manslaughter instead of murder.

Another excellent example of how an old law really paid dividends was when Buford Pusser, the Tennessee sheriff of *Walking Tall* fame, had a serious problem with a crooked judge. There really wasn't much Buford could do under the circumstances, so in frustration he pored over the law books in his office. He discovered an antiquated law that gave the sheriff the duty of assigning the offices of judges and other people who worked in the courthouse.

One Saturday, the wily lawman reassigned his foe to a new office. When the judge came to work on Monday morning, he saw his old office had been stripped of everything. Livid with rage, he asked around and was subsequently led to the men's restroom. There sat his desk and his file cabinets—and there they stayed.

In Manhattan, Kansas, a shoe store manager can eject a customer who proves to have odoriferous feet when trying on a pair of boots. As a test, one could take it on himself to violate this ordinance and see what happens.

In one experiment, a clever chap, on a visit to Louisiana, attempted to prove it's actually a misdemeanor "to goad or harass skunks." But the saucy little animals, unwilling to cooperate, took the law into their own paws and ruined one of his best suits. Ever since then, the fellow has been less interested in proving or disproving the authenticity of certain kinds of animal legislation.

Numerous other odd animal-related laws abound. For example, political candidates aren't allowed to show off, in an effort to garner votes, by riding a horse backwards in Strawberry, Arkansas. A fellow must remove his hat when coming face-to-face with a cow on any road in Fruithill, Kentucky. And legislators in Massachusetts passed a bill forbidding goats from wearing trousers.

For many of our strange laws, a solid reason originally brought them into existence. Take the old, seemingly absurd, Texas statute that still makes carrying a pair of pliers a felony offense. Only a few years ago this tool was used effectively by rustlers to snip a rancher's fence and swipe some of his cattle.

Customs and morals dictated many strange laws, yet when times changed, no one even thought of repealing them. Thus in the state of Washington, women still aren't permitted to walk into a lounge, bar, or tavern unless accompanied by a man. Store window decorators in Atlanta must always pull down the shades while dressing or disrobing their mannequins. And in Oakwood, Illinois, a woman isn't allowed to be seen on the streets unless she's wearing a petticoat.

Romance has always come under legal scrutiny. A man in Connecticut can't write love letters to his

7

girlfriend if her mother forbids this kind of activity. Firemen in Huntington, West Virginia, can't flirt with a woman who strolls past the firehouse. And in Maryland, if a man makes six visits to a woman's home, he's as good as hitched.

Kissing babies or married women in public by a candidate running for public office is prohibited in Barnetts Crossroads, Alabama. A man can legally direct profanity at his wife—if he lives in Delaware. However, a man in Virginia is not allowed to curse and berate his wife except in a whisper. Then it's okay.

In matters of health, as well as hearth, lawmakers have ruled sternly at times. It's strictly against the law for a campaigning politician to sneeze while getting on or off a train in Cooleemee, North Carolina. Residents of Roseburg, Oregon, aren't allowed to take a bath unless they are wearing "a suitable dress reaching from the neck to the knees." And in Amarillo, Texas, it's against the law for anyone to bathe on the streets during business hours.

Considering that most laws are made in haste, many old ones remain amazingly sound. There's an statute in Kansas, for example, that makes it unlawful for a candidate for public office to give away cigars on election day. An ordinance in Charleston, South Carolina, compels prisoners to pay the police one dollar for the privilege of riding to jail in a paddy wagon. And in Denver, Colorado, any person who is found to be "smelly" can't ride on a streetcar.

Yet many other laws appear to have no rhyme or reason. For example, politicians on the campaign trail in Lawton, Oklahoma, can't be "booed" but can be "hissed" while making a speech. A New York State father cannot diaper his baby. And a Bostonian can't own a dog more than ten inches in height.

These and other antique laws will, hopefully, eventually be repealed. But meanwhile, politicians running for office in Georgia can't slap a man on the back while campaigning. Couples in Los Angeles can't dance together unless they're married. Motorists driving in Youngstown, Ohio, are forbidden to run out of gas. No one can feed a dog whiskey when in Joplin, Missouri. And waitresses in New Jersey can't work while wearing transparent skirts.

"No person shall be permitted, under any pretext whatever, to come nearer than fifty feet of any door or window of any polling room, from the opening of the polls until the completion of the count and the certification of the returns." (Arkansas statute)

2

Laws in New England

Profanity is never heard in any magnitude around Kingston, Rhode Island. An ordinance passed in 1897 prohibits the use of "indecent, immoral, obscene, vulgar, or insulting language in the presence or hearing of women or children."

And watch what you say when in Vermont! No person is allowed to "profoundly curse and swear upon arriving at the age of discretion."

New Hampshire legislators had to think really long and hard before passing this unusual traffic stopper: "Any vehicles meeting at an intersection must stop. Each must wait for the other to pass. Neither can proceed until the other is gone."

A woman living in Sanford, Maine, must be cautious when going out in the rain. According to the local law, she must not be so bold as to raise her skirts more than six inches to avoid puddles on the street.

To be legal for sale in Connecticut, pickles must remain unbroken and bounce when dropped from one foot above a solid oak table. Any pickle that breaks or doesn't bounce when dropped twelve inches is considered to be illegal. It can't be sold anywhere in the United States.

Steamed lobster and all kinds of other delectable seafood dishes are popular throughout the New England states. And special laws sometimes govern the making of certain dishes. Boston, for example, actually passed an ordinance prohibiting the addition of tomatoes when one is making up a batch of delicious clam chowder.

A law was long ago passed in Bangor, Maine, which barred snow removal from all public roads. This 1850s ordinance was passed because plowing the snow off the roads interfered with children's sleigh riding. Similar legislation was also passed in many other towns and cities throughout the United States.

Balancing the budget in New Hampshire never was an easy task. Dating from the rule of King George III, the New Hampshire constitution required the accounts of the state to be kept in shillings and pence.

How does one person entice another person's bees? Someone in Connecticut knows the answer to this

11

question, because legislators there passed a special law prohibiting anyone from "enticing the bees of a neighbor."

Men in Pittsfield, Massachusetts, aren't allowed to snore loudly except under certain conditions: the bedroom window must always be tightly closed and securely locked, and the noise from the snoring must not be discernible more than ten feet away.

Sky divers won't have much fun in Maine. Nor can any of the military airborne units get in much practice. The law in Maine prohibits people from stepping out of an airplane while it is still in the air.

A woman should be mighty careful about kicking her husband out of the house in Providence, Rhode Island. According to the law, if the husband refuses to come back, she's the deserter, not he!

Baths are the center of attention in some areas of Vermont. For example, in Morrisville, no one can legally take a bath or a shower unless they first obtain permission from the Board of Selectmen.

Having trouble with your landlord? Watch yourself in Rumford, Maine. You may be able to slap, kick, punch, or spit on your landlord! But a city ordinance was passed that stops a renter from biting a landlord.

An old ordinance in Attleboro, Massachusetts, makes kisses an important part of courtship. And those same kisses could spell disaster for an unwary lover. "Ten kisses," in front of other people, according to the law, "undeniably equals a valid engagement."

Women in Keene, New Hampshire, are extremely limited as to how they can take care of their shoes. No female is allowed to polish her shoes on a Saturday morning "before going shopping in town or visiting with lady friends."

What a married woman wears when she leaves the house is carefully covered by law in Torrington, Connecticut. The law prohibits such a woman from going for a drive while wearing a housecoat, while attired in lingerie, or while wrapped in a robe. Single women, since the law doesn't mention them, are apparently free to do as they please!

Don't expect to be treated nicely in Middlebury, Vermont, if you pull off the street and try to catch forty winks in the trunk of your car. Local lawmakers passed a law banning citizens from napping in the trunk of a car—if the trunk lid is "partially open to

13

public view." Guess it's fine to doze in a trunk if you get in and carefully close the lid before putting on your pajamas.

Abandoning puppies at the local dump in subzero weather is illegal in Rochester, New Hampshire. Violators of this law may be sentenced to spend two nights in freezing weather at the same dump. The law forbids the guilty party from building a shelter, but the culprit is allowed to dress as warmly as possible. And the puppies had better bundle up, too.

Every hotel owner in Boston has a special responsibility to his guests. The law requires that the hotel owner make provisions to "put up and properly bed down" the horse ridden by a guest.

Crooks will have a difficult time in little Beanville, Vermont. An old law clearly states that anyone driving a car into the community who "intends to rob a bank, or injure or murder someone, must first register with the Chief of Police or other pertinent legal authority." To commit such crimes without first registering is against the law.

Actresses in New London, Connecticut, can't be seen on the streets, in a restaurant, shopping in a store, or anywhere else. A local ordinance forbids actresses to appear in public! Nothing in the law mentions actors.

A person can be arrested for giving bread crumbs to birds in a park on Sunday if this is done within the boundaries of Biddeford, Maine, while church services are being conducted. Birds in the park may be legally fed in the afternoon after church has let out.

Just about everyone in Fitchburg, Massachusetts, loves their coffee in the morning. Nevertheless, an old ordinance prohibits anyone from giving a baby lukewarm coffee to drink.

Tennis partners of the opposite sex in Warwick, Rhode Island, are forbidden by local legislation to stop playing and begin kissing while on a tennis court within the city limits. There is an exception to this rule: one kiss only is okay so long as the female is seen to be standing within a well-lighted area of the tennis court. The woman will be fined a dollar for each kiss over the legally allowable one. There's no penalty for the wayward fellow!

Don't try to take your girlfriend or your wife on a Sunday drive in the country around Lebanon, New Hampshire. There's an old law that prohibits a man from asking a female to go for a ride alone with him on the Sabbath. No woman is ever allowed to get into a man's automobile unless she's accompanied by a minimum of two other female friends.

Anyone who desires may chew tobacco in Brattleboro, Vermont. But the law says a man cannot "expectorate against the wind" while chewing in a public place or while around any other people. Perhaps a woman can expectorate however she wishes, since the law specifically mentions only men.

It would certainly be better not to have the audacity to call a police officer a pig in Waterville, Maine. Those who do this can be made to spend three hours sitting in a pigsty with a bunch of wallowing hogs. Such a sentence is given by the authorities in an effort to teach the lawbreaker the difference between police officers and pigs.

A knife-throwing expert in Wallingford, Connecticut, has few restrictions covering his profession. Knives may be tossed at a woman in a bathing suit or just about anyone else for that matter. But there is one notable restriction called for in the law. The fellow can't practice throwing his knives at a man attired in a natty pinstriped suit!

Native Americans can live in the community and they can grocery shop, buy homes, socialize—but there's a limit as to what Hatfield, Massachusetts, is willing to let Native Americans do. Per this old law, they are prohibited from pitching their "wigwams" anywhere "on the town commons."

It's strictly against the law in Bristol, Rhode Island, for a woman to be found shaving her legs while driving to work in the morning. And a woman can't shave her legs in the backseat of an automobile while attending a drive-in movie. Guess she's allowed to commit this dastardly deed if she's sitting in the front seat, since the law mentions only the back.

One town in New Hampshire has an unusual bathing ordinance. Every man in Kidderville who decides to take a bath in a bathtub must do so only while wearing clothing enough "to entirely cover his body from head to foot." Evidently women are allowed to get in a tub and bathe while partially or completely disrobed. And should a man decide to take a bath other than in a tub, he can do so in an unclothed state.

Anyone who digs up a mayflower, the Massachusetts state flower, is breaking the law! A fine of $50 is levied on those who happen to get caught. But should a Massachusetts citizen get caught digging up a mayflower while wearing any sort of disguise, the fine is automatically doubled!

17

Working women in St. Albans, Vermont, should always bathe before reporting to work each day. No female, married or single, is allowed to take a bath in the office. It must be okay for women to shower on the job, since the law makes no mention of this.

Some places are particular regarding the kind of bathtub a person can legally install in his or her home. Jackman, Maine, lawmakers don't seem to care if a tub is round or square or red or yellow. Only one thing really matters. Every bathtub must, by law, have four legs! Should a tub have no legs, then it's illegal to install it inside a home.

Women in Waterbury, Connecticut, are prohibited from applying makeup while walking or standing on any street in the community. Nor can a female be seen fixing her hair, adjusting her pantyhose, or putting on lipstick while she eats in a restaurant or is shopping in a store.

Littleton, New Hampshire, has an unusual law on the books regarding the Sabbath. Single guys and gals are banned from going house hunting on Sunday. Any unattached male or female who takes part in such harmless activities can be arrested, fined, and given a

18

jail term. The only exceptions are people who are either widowed or divorced.

The law in Shaftsbury, Vermont, bans all local citizens from "driving ugly automobiles." Ugly cars aren't allowed within three miles of the city limits. Anyone stopped and found guilty of driving an ugly automobile will be fined a minimum of $5 and serve up to three days in jail.

Women who rent will have to be a little more careful when living within the boundaries of Lewiston, Maine. It's illegal for a female renter to bite her landlord during an argument over the rent. And it's against the law for her to bite other renters as well.

Driving through Massachusetts while on vacation? Watch for the highway patrolmen! They'll be carefully checking to see if you're driving with both hands on the wheel. This law isn't enforced to stop a fellow from hugging his girlfriend or vice versa; nobody really cares anything about that. It's enforced to stop drivers from taking a hand off the steering wheel in order to operate a CB radio.

Some communities have specific days on which children may be given a bath. Hopkins Hollow, Rhode Island, for example, has an ordinance that allows only once-a-week bathing. This odd law prohibits anyone from bathing a child except on a Saturday night. Evidently showers aren't prohibited, since the ordinance specifies only a bath.

Don't put a strip of tape over the official state motto on your license plates if you live in New Hampshire. Covering the words "Live Free or Die" is against the law. The charge will be "misusing" your license plates.

A law was once passed in Pasoag, Rhode Island, which forbid vegetable peddlers from crying their wares on the streets of the community. But one ingenious peddler quickly found a way to do business as usual. He simply named his horse Cabbages and covered his route shouting, "Whoa, Cabbages! Whoa, Cabbages!"

The elderly once had a major problem in Maine. The legislature passed a law authorizing the SPCA to "put old dogs, cats, and people out of their misery."

People who ride trains to and from work in Connecticut have little to be concerned about. According to the law, the railroad has to pay each passenger $25 if they are delayed for more than five minutes by a standing train.

> "A lodger shall not be lodged for more than seven consecutive nights unless he shall have taken a bath." (Boston ordinance)

3

Mid-Atlantic States' Laws

One Pennsylvania community came up with a rather novel idea in order to warn drivers of their strictly enforced speed law. They put up a unique sign to induce potential speeders to slow down—or else! It's posted on all roads entering a suburb just outside of Pittsburgh: "Neville Township Reminds You! Thirty Days Hath September, April, June, and November—and Anyone Exceeding Our Speed Limit."

Smithtown, New York, had a major problem with barking dogs. A law was passed by the town board. Dogs were banned from continuously barking for a period of more than fifteen minutes. Prolonged yelping brings a $50 fine for a first offense. A second offense costs a $100 fine. And dogs who try barking a third time will bring a $500 fine and fifteen days in jail. The only problem encountered was finding a way to explain this ordinance to all the dogs in the community.

One law in Maryland could be construed to be somewhat biased toward women. This Howard County legislation is clear—or is it? "Females in heat must be properly confined so as not to entice males from home." The people who wrote this law forgot to mention that it was directed at female dogs!

Claytop, Delaware, is certainly the place to live for married men. If a fellow's wife decides to leave him, she may find herself facing a serious problem. The guy can follow her down the street and remove her clothing, one item at a time. According to this loony law, everything the woman has is legally his property.

People who are driving in Princeton, New Jersey, will have to be super careful. The unusual ordinance specifies: "Motorists may not back their automobiles into trees in public places." How about trucks?

There's a most interesting ordinance to be found in Pottstown, Pennsylvania. Community officials are required to check all fire hydrants. What's so unusual about this? They must do it one hour before every fire starts.

This next one must have been a forerunner to Michael Jackson's moonwalking. Newburgh, New York, has an ordinance regarding concerts held within the city

23

limits. No person in attendance can walk backward while eating peanuts or popcorn within earshot of the music.

No one is allowed to use profanity anywhere in Maryland while standing within six feet of a sheriff or a sheriff's deputy. The fine—twenty-five cents for each swear word used—is automatic and is to be paid on the spot.

Delaware lawmakers even legislated what their citizens had to wear at night when walking along a road or highway. But they forgot to specify that it had to be clothing. Here's the unusual wording of the law: "All pedestrians on a highway after sundown must wear white cloth to make them visible to motorists." Chalk one up for the Klan!

No one in Browns Mills, New Jersey, is allowed to "molest a man who is snoring," even if his snoring "annoys the neighbors." But there's a catch here! The snoring noise "must always be accompanied by sleep."

Altoona, Pennsylvania, passed a special rock 'n' roll ordinance. Local lawmakers became fed up with this kind of pop music and decided to do something about the problem. A fine was imposed for singing, humming or whistling any rock 'n' roll tune between the hours of 6:00 A.M. and 10:00 P.M.

Here's another one of those impossible-to-obey driving laws. This weird one is found in New York: "Two vehicles which are passing each other in opposite directions shall have the right of way."

An old law in Baltimore doesn't pull any punches when it comes to the kind of milk allowed to be sold in the city. The only milk deemed to be suitable is "pure, unadulterated, unsophisticated, and wholesome."

Leap year can be bad for the male population of Dover, Delaware. Why? Because no man is allowed to propose to his sweetie during leap year. But should she instead propose to him, the fellow must immediately accept—or face a fine!

House-to-house salesmen must beware of plying their trade within the boundaries of Bridgewater, New Jersey. A local ordinance declares: "No person shall disturb the occupant of any house by knocking on the door or ringing the bell. Nor shall a person yell, stomp, pound on, or kick a door to get the attention of the occupant or occupants."

25

Need to hire a baby-sitter? People in Carlisle, Pennsylvania, are rather well protected by an unusual kind of ordinance. It's illegal for a baby-sitter to eat all of the food in the employer's refrigerator while being paid to take care of the children. Baby-sitters must always have written permission before freely snacking.

The lowly pickle was the object of some special oddball legislation in New York some years ago. Pickles, for some unexplainable reason, can't be sold by themselves in a restaurant. They must "accompany a meal as a substitute for butter." Did those oddball New York legislators ever try spreading pickles on a slice of bread?

Hazlettville, Delaware, passed an ordinance some years ago in an effort to better handle some of the more common medical problems found in children. The law requires that all kids playing out-of-doors with a cold must wear a sign saying, "Beware! I have a cold!"

It's illegal to keep anyone in jail on the Sabbath in Kulpmont, Pennsylvania. Prisoners who find themselves behind bars on a Sunday can demand to be freed. They must simply yell, "I want out, in the name of the law!"

A woman in New Jersey can still be prosecuted under an old law if she assaults one of her neighbors. She can be tried as "a common scold and disturber of the peace of the neighborhood." The traditional penalty in days gone by was simply "a public dunking."

The law in Annapolis, Maryland, is really tough on taxi drivers. Cabbies are prohibited from locking a female passenger in their taxi. Such an act can bring a $500 fine and three years' probation!

Buy a brand-new vehicle and it's not running just right? Having problems with that used car you picked up on a local dealer's lot? Either way, there's not much a person can do in Washington, D.C., if they inadvertently purchased a lemon. It's actually against the law there to paint lemons all over your automobile in an effort to let everyone know how you were taken advantage of by a particular dealer.

When the first automobiles began to chug their way through the streets of America's towns and cities, lawmakers were plagued by citizens who demanded protection from the dangers of the horseless carriage. Most of these fears came from a lack of knowledge. But regardless of why these laws were passed, they're still on the books in many states. One of the strangest pieces of legislation around today is the one in Delaware, enacted when the automobile first came to that state. The statute reads in part: "Any man driving a motor vehicle on a street or road or highway after the sun has set, is to pull over once each mile traveled. He must shoot a rocket into the air as a warning signal to cows and horses on the road ahead. The motorist is required to wait a minimum of ten minutes for livestock to be cleared from the road. He may then proceed on his journey."

Until recently, dwarf bowling and dwarf tossing were both highly popular sports in the Empire State. But both of these unique activities have now been made illegal. No longer can anyone in New York legally strap a dwarf to a skateboard and roll him at a set of bowling pins. Nor are lawmakers allowing the sport of dwarf tossing. Citizens are prohibited from strapping a dwarf in a special harness and then hurling him toward a mattress!

Comic book lovers, beware of Rayville, Maryland. A strange local ordinance bans anglers from reading comic books while fishing on a lake or river.

Couples in McClellandville, Delaware, shouldn't take unnecessary risks by hugging, kissing, or just plain holding hands when out walking or shopping. A local ordinance prohibits "any unseemly displays of affection" on the streets or in any public place of business.

A person can smoke all they want while touring around Washington, D.C. But be careful when it's necessary to flick those cigarette ashes. It is against the law to flick cigarette ashes into the Potomac River!

Own one or more frogs? Like to enter them in a frog-jumping contest? You'll have no problem in Newark, New Jersey, except in one specific situation. An old ordinance prohibits holding frog-jumping contests in nightclubs or taverns where alcoholic beverages are served.

Holiday Inn, the Hilton, and others must look out if they're doing business in Pennsylvania. Some old legislation specifically requires: "Every innkeeper must provide good, clean, and moral entertainment for his guests."

Husbands in Branchville, New Jersey, can't go fishing without the spouse along at any time unless they've been married for more than twelve months. The penalty: "Imprisonment in the city jail for not more than one (1) week or by a fine of $25 or by both fine and imprisonment."

Don't go to Salisbury, Maryland, if you'd like to feed your horse in a quiet park. There's a strict law against this kind of activity! And you can't even allow your horse to take a drink from any decorative fountain in any park or playground. It'll cost you a fine and five days in jail.

Washington, D.C., has a unique slacks law. A woman can't attend a public sporting event while wearing slacks. The penalty? She must walk around the city with a sign saying she'll never again break the law. Females must "always proudly attire themselves as women."

Women in New York aren't allowed to knit at home and then sell their goods to friends, relatives, or even in a flea market. Such activities are against the law for females of all ages. Maybe men can knit at home?

Smokers may end up having a terrible nicotine fit while attending a funeral in Taylors Bridge, Delaware. A local ordinance prohibits any person from smoking a pipe, cigar, or cigarettes while in a cemetery during a funeral.

Be careful when out hunting or simply walking in the Pennsylvania countryside. Don't accidentally step on a snake and kill it. No one, under any circumstances, is allowed to kill a snake unless the snake first bites the individual!

New Castle, Delaware, has an odd antinecking law on the books. No one is allowed to exchange kisses while out walking their dog. Also, a couple may not even hold hands in public while holding a dog on a leash.

People in Chestertown, Maryland, are prohibited from playing a radio loud enough that it can be heard fifty feet away. Nor can kids or anyone else practice drums or play a bugle, piano, or organ except under the same sound limitations.

Strikers in Upper St. Clair, Pennsylvania, can't snore while snoozing on the picket line. Snoozing by itself is no infraction of the law. But a person who snores while picketing will be charged with "not picketing peacefully."

Cucumber lovers won't want to visit Pennsville, New Jersey. Cucumbers, for some unexplainable reason, came under fire in this community. The law prohibits anyone from selling baskets of fresh cucumbers within the town limits.

If you happen to have a farm around Slaterville, New York, be extremely careful how you spend your free time. Trying to sell farm produce in the gymnasium before a girls' basketball game or a volleyball game is against the law!

Looks as if horses will always be an absolute necessity around Punxsutawney, Pennsylvania. To travel through this community, an automobile must always be pulled by a team of horses supplied by the local farmers' co-op.

"A railway company which negligently throws a passenger from a crowded car onto the trestle is held liable for injury to a relative who, in going to his rescue, falls through the trestle." (New York common law)

4

Laws in the South

Every able-bodied family man in South Carolina has a duty to protect his wife and children. An old law requires that such a man must "carry two loaded horse pistols, in good working order," whenever he is taking the family to church or to any church-related activities.

An old 1864 divorce law still exists in Georgia. As silly as this may sound, a woman can actually divorce her spouse should he ever decide to join the military and go off to war.

Railroad people must not have been very well liked in West Virginia of yesteryear. It was illegal for an official of a railroad to be a member of the state legislature. This political fact of life was actually included in West Virginia's original constitution.

It's illegal in Fayetteville, Tennessee, for a girl to do cartwheels while crossing a street. Nor can any youngster be seen walking across a street on his hands.

Here is one of the stranger aspects of Tennessee's criminal code: It's a felony for one citizen to point a loaded gun at another citizen. But pointing a loaded gun at a police officer is only a misdemeanor! You figure out the thinking behind this one.

Some women in Laurinburg, North Carolina, never seem to learn from experience. In order to protect these females from themselves, an ordinance was hastily written and passed. According to the law, no woman in Laurinburg is allowed to marry the same fellow more than seven times!

Cabbies must be rather selective in choosing their fares according to the law in Magnolia, Arkansas. An unusual ordinance spells it out: "Cab drivers may not knowingly carry a person of questionable or bad character to his or her destination."

A few people are just that way and won't bother bathing whatever the circumstances. So the Kentucky legislature took it upon themselves to pass a law to make these bathless individuals toe the line. According to the statute, any person who lives in Kentucky must bathe a minimum of once each year. A citizen who refuses to take an annual bath can be forcibly given one in a creek, river, lake, or spring by his or her neighbors.

People can walk to church in Honaker, Virginia. And they can come on the back of a horse or in a carriage or a buckboard. But there's one thing people can't do in Honaker—they can't be seen riding a mule to church!

It may not seem fair to other citizens, but this is the way it is in South Carolina: A butcher can't legally be selected to sit on a jury in a murder trial.

Gainesville, Georgia, is widely known as the "Chicken Capital of the World." As could be expected, a law exists that prohibits the "eating of Southern fried chicken with a fork." This ordinance could fit smoothly in every Southern community where fried chicken, long before the Colonel came on the scene, has *always* been "finger-lickin' good." And no sane person would ever consider using a fork to eat it.

Are you a woman in Whitesville, Kentucky, who really wants to get married to that fellow of your dreams? Propose to him if you wish, but be careful as to when you decide to do this. A local law declares

35

that a woman is guilty of misconduct if she proposes to a man during leap year!

Arkansas has a law similar in silliness to those found in many other states. Railroads that obey this statute would really have a problem keeping a time schedule of any kind. The strange legislation reads: "Two approaching trains must both stop at crossings. Neither can proceed until the other has passed."

The law in Wheeling, West Virginia, doesn't accept the practice of witchcraft as having any sort of validity. Therefore, anyone caught playing around with witchcraft in any fashion can be arrested. The charge is: "Fraudulently pretending to exercise witchcraft."

The wearing of corsets is still required in many areas of the country. This is especially true in places like Shelby, North Carolina, whenever a woman is dressed in "clothing that firmly hugs her body."

Corset wearing is also a must in Russellville, Arkansas. Why? Because it's against the law for "a married or unmarried woman's body parts to quiver" as she walks down a street in the community.

Every business in the city of Nashville must have at least one hitching post out in front of the establishment. Despite the hitching post requirement for the convenience of horses, Nashville city fathers must not care much for mules. An ordinance prohibits anyone from tying a mule to one of these hitching posts.

Motorists will have to be careful when driving after dark around Mufreesboro, Arkansas. An old law bans anyone from operating a "motorized contraption" within the city limits after the sun goes down.

Kentucky has some pretty good ideas when it comes to who shouldn't be able to marry whom within the state. But why is it necessary to have a law to tell the average Kentuckian what he or she already knows? One old statute says: "A man shall not marry the grandmother of his wife."

Pedestrians must be especially careful in Virginia. If struck by a moving automobile, the pedestrian—*not* the driver—is subject to a fine.

Tobacco auctioneers in Asheboro, North Carolina, could have an insurmountable problem. An old ordinance forbids tobacco auctioneers from "chanting indistinctly."

According to an old South Carolina statute, a person must first obtain permission from the principal "to

37

act in an obnoxious manner on the campus of a girls' school." It must be okay to act obnoxious on the campus of a boys' school since the law mentions only girls.

Memphis, Tennessee, city fathers passed an ordinance prohibiting frogs from croaking after 11:00 P.M. No mention is made of this problem: who will explain the law to the poor frogs?

Horses appear to be treated with the greatest respect in some areas of the country. For example, everyone is required to bow from the waist when meeting a horse and buggy on a road or in a field around Maysville, West Virginia. Why? Because it's the law!

Bentonville, Arkansas, isn't what anyone would ever call a busy or a noisy place. Still, so as not to scare horses, local politicos many years ago passed an ordinance against sneezing in public. Evidently spurred on by the excitement of passing a new law, they also added other noisy activities to the banned list. Now, whenever you visit Bentonville, be warned that it's not only against the law to sneeze in the streets or any public place, it is also illegal to sharpen an axe, beat a drum, whistle, preach, spank a baby, gargle, burp, or snore.

Taking care of your garbage is certainly a necessity. But in Staunton, Virginia, it's against the law to put out the trash more than eighteen hours before it's to be picked up. Nor can a person sneak out at night and put his garbage in front of a neighbor's house.

Charleston, South Carolina, surely must have its share of nuts! But why a ridiculous ordinance prohibiting the eating of nuts on a city bus? The maximum penalties for munching nuts on a bus are sixty days in jail and a $500 fine! Politicians in Charleston certainly take their nuts seriously, don't they?

No officer of the law can arrest a minister while the preacher is conducting a church service anywhere in Kentucky. The law reads: "Any officer who arrests, or attempts to arrest . . . any clergyman while he is publicly preaching . . . in any religious assembly shall be fined not less than ten nor more than fifty dollars."

It's illegal in North Carolina to publish a motorist's prayer on any highway map sold or given away in the state. Why are such maps banned? Because, said the court, by printing a prayer on the official map, the state is seen to "impermissibly sponsor religious activity."

Trains passing through Arkansas communities have always been governed by a strange piece of loony legislation. This law requires a train to toot its whistle once when approaching a single-story farmhouse. And the whistle must be tooted twice when coming to a two-story farmhouse. Imagine what it would be like to hear it toot when passing a skyscraper around Little Rock or West Memphis.

Inhabitants of the small village of Gassaway, West Virginia, won't be waking up to the sounds of nocturnal cowbells. According to a local ordinance, cows may wear their clanging bells only during daylight hours. The "offending instruments must be removed from their necks between 8:00 P.M. and 7:00 A.M."

There never really was much to do in Bells, Tennessee, and the city aldermen made sure there'd be even less. A law was passed to ban the three "beer halls" from the little town in Crockett County. Davy Crockett himself probably is rolling over in his grave over this one!

A bill was passed in the North Carolina legislature making the gray squirrel the official state animal. One vocal objector to this bill may have had a good point when he declared: "I would like to say that an animal that can bury nuts could be dangerous to this General Assembly."

40

People in Virginia have to be mighty careful how they bathe. According to an old piece of loony legislation, it's illegal to take a bath in a tub if the tub happens to be located in any room attached to the house.

Anyone under the age of sixteen in Covington, Kentucky, can't be seen on the streets alone after 10:30 P.M. between May and October. The curfew time changes to 9:30 P.M. between November and April. If a youth under sixteen is on the streets and unaccompanied by an adult, the parents are given an automatic $50 fine!

Watch how you act around a cop in Parkersburg, West Virginia. It's against the law to "tiptoe up behind a policeman" and shout "Boo!" Anyone breaking this law will receive a $5 fine.

Don't sit in your car and try to sneak a romantic kiss or two while waiting for the light to change in Nashville. Kissing at an intersection in the Country Music Capital of the World is a misdemeanor and punishable by a $15 fine. So much for young love!

Here's a great piece of loony legislation for all people who like to spend their spare time barking at passing trucks. This ordinance comes out of Morganton, North Carolina: "Barking at a dog truck while it is

41

being driven by a state employee . . . is showing disrespect toward a state official." Sounds just a little bit like Orwell's *Animal Farm*.

Anyone who shoots a gun at a buddy in Georgia must exercise a fair degree of caution. The law reads: "Those who shoot at friends for amusement ought to warn them first that it is mere sport."

Male students in Buckhannon, West Virginia, aren't allowed to "pat or pinch the posterior" of a female student in the school lounge. To pinch or pat the buttocks of a passing female could bring a $119 fine.

Some police officers in Norfolk, Virginia, face a problem most cops never run into. They can't buy guns! Politicians in Norfolk lowered the age limit for police officers from twenty-one to eighteen. Everything went smoothly until the young officers tried to follow a departmental regulation that required them to carry a gun when off duty. Though the police department furnished their service revolvers, officers are required to buy their own off-duty weapons. And according to Virginia law, no one under twenty-one can buy a handgun or bullets.

Don't try fooling around with your meters, or bypassing them in an effort to steal gas, water, or electricity in Tennessee. Besides the possibility of criminal prosecution, the law provides that the utility company has the right to bill the customer for three times the amount of power or water stolen.

Men in Anderson, South Carolina, had better watch out. It's illegal for a man to bite a strange woman on her buttocks, or to kiss her at all. Such activities could bring as much as a twenty-year prison term.

"Each and every bathing beach guard must be seen wearing a bright red body-covering bathing suit attached to a sturdy leather harness and a lifeline 200 feet long." (Georgia statute)

5

Southwestern Sunbelt Laws

Mickey Mouse prohibited from running for public office in Comal County, Texas? Yes! Because, according to authorities: "Mickey Mouse is not and has not been a resident of Comal County for six months as required by law . . . Mickey Mouse is . . . very probably an unpardoned felon and is, therefore, under the laws of Texas, ineligible to hold office."

Never steal a bar of soap if you're in Mojave County, Arizona. The law for soap stealing metes out an unusual penalty. The thief is required to bathe with the bar of soap until it's all used up. A police officer is assigned the job of watching to be sure the penalty is properly carried out.

Do you really like horned lizards, often called horned toads? Want to take one home to raise as a pet? You'd have to ask the governor—if you're in New Mexico. The law prohibits taking any "live horned toads out of the state" without first obtaining permission from the governor.

Every "drinking engineer or conductor or driver" is guilty of a misdemeanor in Oklahoma. The old law covers: "Every person who, while in charge, as engineer, of a locomotive engine, or while acting as conductor or driver upon a railroad train or car . . . drawn by horses."

Banana peelings can't be tossed on the streets in Waco, Texas? Yes! And it's not an environmental issue, nor is it one dealing with throwing garbage on a street. It's simply that a horse could step on a banana peel and slip.

Lingerie may be shown in store windows throughout the community of Chambers, Arizona. But the law says it "must be done with discretion, modesty, and propriety."

Are you a guy who has grown weary of your fiancée? Be careful if you're in Brownfield, Texas, and intend to end the relationship. No man in Brownfield is allowed to jilt a woman. Should he do this, according to the law, he must leave town within six hours or go to jail for thirty days. Brownfield women must be

45

able to jilt their boyfriends at will, since the law specifically mentions only men.

When crossing the bridge upon entering or leaving Wickenburg, Arizona, a driver will see a permanent bronze sign that says: NO FISHING FROM BRIDGE. Yes, the law in Wickenburg prohibits anyone from dropping a line over the side of this bridge. But there's a problem here. No water is to be found under the bridge!

Here's one for baseball fans, a sport Mickey Mantle did much for in his home state of Oklahoma. Visiting ballplayers are prohibited from "hitting a ball over the home team's fence or out of the park," when playing a game in Muskogee. This ordinance has never really been enforced, nor was it ever meant to be. It was passed in jest as a show of local team support by the city council. A prominent Muskogee attorney explained: "Sometimes, during a game, when a visiting ballplayer hits a home run, a deputy in uniform goes out on the field and issues a citation to the guilty player as he crosses home plate. The crowd loves it. But we never fine the fellow or consider putting him in jail. It's all done in a friendly spirit."

Paradise for snuff dippers surely must be El Paso, Texas! Any business in this beautiful city—stores, banks, hotels, railroad station, nightclubs, and saloons—is breaking the law if it doesn't supply spittoons for the customers. Even local churches are required by law to provide spittoons for all of their tobacco-chewing, snuff-dipping members.

New Mexico is especially kind to its convicts. Each man or woman, upon being released from the state penitentiary, is given an outfit of new clothing, a horse, and a saddle.

Women and children in Oklahoma are protected from the wrath of a man's vulgarities. The law says: "If any person shall utter or speak any obscene or lascivious language or word . . . in the presence of females, or in the presence of children under ten years of age, he shall be liable to a fine of not more than one hundred dollars, or imprisonment for not more than thirty days, or both." Cursing and swearing in public are also outlawed.

Arizona isn't a state where any sane illicit drug dealer would want to ply his trade. Why? Because Arizona law specifies that illegal drug dealers are required to register with the state before going into the business of selling cocaine, marijuana, heroin, smack, or what-have-you.

The Oklahoma legislature passed a fluke of a law regarding divorced women. According to this legislation, such a woman gets *everything*—even the personal possessions acquired by her husband prior to their marriage. The bill was originally designed to give a woman back her maiden name after a divorce was finalized. But somehow a clause was slipped in that gave the woman not only her maiden name, but also "all the property, lands . . . owned by either party before marriage or acquired by either party in their own right after such marriage, and not previously disposed of."

The number of courts and judges required by law in Texas is astounding. The constitution of Texas calls for five times as many courts and judges as serve the infinitely larger population of Great Britain. And all this was adopted during buckskin days, when Dallas was too small even to be counted in the census.

No man in the state of Oklahoma is allowed to "falsely and maliciously . . . impute to any female, married or unmarried, a want of chastity . . ." In other words, a man can't accuse a woman of being a nonvirgin, or of not being sexually pure. Such an accusation can bring a fine of up to $500 and up to ninety days in jail.

48

Taxes, taxes, and still more crazy taxes—is there no end in sight? Apparently not for a bachelor living in Clifton, Arizona. Unmarried males must pay a special $1 tax each year as a penalty for remaining single. The ordinance doesn't apply to females.

A husband in Alamogordo, New Mexico, may find himself in trouble with the authorities. An old ordinance holds a husband responsible for any crimes his wife commits in his presence. The one exception? Murder!

Most traffic offenses in the state of Texas require the arrest and jailing of the lawbreaker. Such offenses include driving with one headlight out, having a broken tail light, etc. But one offense doesn't require that the driver go to jail when given a citation—speeding! A speeder simply gets a ticket and then heads merrily on his way.

Horses are extremely popular in New Mexico. But an old ordinance governs the trading of horses in the communities of Lordsburg and Clayton. Local citizens aren't allowed to set up a tent and camp alongside a road or a highway in order to trade their horses, or to trade for someone else's horses.

Where in the Unites States could a person find a law regarding "domino parlors"? Look no farther than colorful Stillwater, Oklahoma! Until recently, Stillwater imposed some rather unique monthly taxes on their business establishments: $2.50 for grocery stores; $2.00 for a beauty shop; and $10.00 on a domino parlor. The money was initially used to pay the salary of Stillwater's one policeman.

A very real law in Tucson, Arizona, reads: "It shall be unlawful for any visiting football team or player to carry, convey, tote, kick, throw, pass, or otherwise transport or propel any inflated pigskin across the University of Arizona goal line or score a safety within the confines of the City of Tucson, County of Pima, State of Arizona." A Tucson detective stated: "The antiscoring ordinance was passed by the City of Tucson in a spirit of fun and goodwill. No football player has ever really been arrested, put in jail, or made to pay the $300 fine. Nor will this law ever be enforced. It was never meant to be. Everybody knows that."

McAlester, Oklahoma, has this wonderfully weird piece of ludicrous legalese to wade through. It reads: "No one shall drive any kind of motorized vehicle while said vehicle is running and while dipping snuff or chewing tobacco." But such loony legislation is certainly appropriate in Oklahoma. After all, this is the state that has warning signs posted on their highways: DO NOT CROSS CENTER MEDIAN. If this doesn't strike you as funny, get out a dictionary and look up the word *median*.

No man, woman, or child in Nacogdoches, Texas, is allowed to crack pecan shells while sitting in a church service. Nor can a churchgoer eat pecans while a minister is preaching the Gospel, during prayer in church, or while the choir is singing hymns.

Men in Holbrook, Arizona, have to be on guard once they start dating one woman on a regular basis. They can't legally go out with another woman unless their steady date first approves. For every dinner a man buys for the other women in his life, he must match this with a similar dinner for his steady partner.

A woman in Farmington, New Mexico, gains a distinct advantage when she gets married. The law allows her to search through her husband's pockets while he soundly snoozes. On the other hand, hubby is never allowed even to sneak a peek in her purse or handbag.

The Klan has an army? Apparently so, at least in the Lone Star State. According to the authorities: "The Klan's primary vehicle for threats, harassment, and intimidation is their military activities and training by and through the Texas Emergency Reserve." And so

51

a law was passed that permanently "barred the Ku Klux Klan from maintaining its own army in Texas."

Don't sit on your boyfriend's lap just because he asks you to. The law in Lawton, Oklahoma, spells it out clearly: "No young woman shall sit on a man's lap without a cushion or a pillow under her."

The law in Pecos, Texas, allows the sheriff to arrest people for "walking or sitting on the wrong side of the street." If the culprit happens to have long hair, he's made to get a haircut. If the culprit sports a beard, he's made to shave! Here's what the Pecos lawman has to say: "Eighty-five percent of all the people in this jail are—were—longhairs. That indicates to me that practically all thugs wear long hair. It's a kind of badge. And their clothes. It's the type of dress that pushers use. So there might be a tendency for my deputies to be suspicious, though certainly they don't put 'em in jail just for long hair."

Teenagers have to be careful when having fun in Tuba City, Arizona. It's illegal for teen fellows to swing on any sign hanging over a city sidewalk. It's also against the law to climb up on a billboard sign and sit.

"Profane swearing" is against the law in Oklahoma. This, per a 1910 law, consists of using "the name of

God, or Jesus Christ, or the Holy Ghost." The punishment for using such profanity is "a fine of one dollar for each offense."

That old radio may not work anymore. It may just be junk. But in Claypool, Arizona, for some unexplainable reason, a person isn't allowed to "willfully destroy an old radio." Any person caught doing this is subject to a fine of one dollar and a possible day in jail.

Couples who love doing the Texas two-step and other popular country-western dances should watch themselves when going out on the town in Socorro, New Mexico. Sweethearts are prohibited from dancing cheek-to-cheek in public. This applies even if the dancing couple happens to be married.

Rabble-rousing adults as well as noisy children can be penalized in Bisbee, Arizona. The law can come down on them should they "bellow, holler, screech, shriek, scream, howl, or yell" and thereby disrupt a ball game, a movie, or any other event attended by others.

> "Insanity is not evidenced when a widow, anxious to marry, shows her love letters from one suitor to another, and boasts constantly about her conquests, both real and those imagined." (Oklahoma common law)

53

6

Laws in the Heartland

The first city in the United States to outlaw the wearing of *midi*skirts was Hanover Park, Illinois. Why such a ban in the first place? Here's the word of the mayor: "We've got some fine-looking women's legs here, and we believe in encouraging them to be seen."

Iowa women are prohibited from going out in public while wearing a corset or a girdle! The old corset-girdle legislation also provided for official state corset-girdle inspectors. These state employees spent their time going around and poking women in the ribs with a forefinger. This is how they determined whether or not she was wearing one.

How does a Minnesota fellow announce his intentions to his girlfriend's parents? According to the law, a hug and a kiss in front of her mother and father, combined with several boxes of candy as gifts to the

young woman, are considered to be enough to indi-
cate his intent.

People in Gary, Indiana, will not allow citizens to
board a streetcar or a bus immediately after chewing
a piece of garlic. Garlic eaters must always wait four
hours before taking a ride on any mode of public
transportation.

Police officers in Rochester, Michigan, really enjoy
some parts of their job. Imagine having to go to the
beach or a local swimming pool and inspect all those
bikini-clad lovelies. Those lucky cops are required to
inspect and approve the outfit worn by any bather at
any given time.

A western cattle drive wouldn't go over well in the
Midwest—certainly not in Peru, Illinois. Here's the
odd ordinance: "No person shall drive along any
public street more than five head of cattle."

Sullivan, Missouri, certainly isn't the ideal place to
have any kind of automobile accident. A city ordinance prohibits anyone other than an actual accident
victim from calling an ambulance in time of an emergency.

It's easier in Massillon, Ohio, to get your chicken at
the Colonel's. A person can't normally just run next

55

door and kill his neighbor's chickens. He can do this only after "getting written permission from the majority of other residents" who live within 500 feet of the chickens.

Being a lumberjack in Wisconsin must be one of the cleanest jobs in the world. Here's an odd piece of legislation affecting the lumbering industry: "Every proprietor of a lumber camp must supply an individual bathtub for each lumberjack in his employ."

Motorists must always be on guard when visiting St. Cloud, Minnesota. Don't *ever* double-park just because you're in a hurry. A conviction for double-parking can bring a sentence of hard labor on a chain gang. Such lawbreakers are fed only bread and water!

Have a fire? Need the fire department in a hurry? Be patient if you happen to be in Fort Madison, Iowa. All firemen are required by law to "practice fire fighting for 15 minutes before attending a fire."

Married men in at least one Michigan community had better be careful how they talk around their spouses. An old ordinance prohibits a man from "swearing and cursing" in front of his wife within the boundaries of Cheboygan.

Kids will enjoy getting a haircut in Bloomington, Indiana. Why? Because barbers can't frighten a child by threatening to cut off an ear while trimming his hair.

Every boarding house and restaurant in Wisconsin must unfailingly obey a special cheese-related statute. They are required to give a free two-thirds of an ounce piece of cheese with every meal costing more than twenty-five cents.

Even the color of an automobile is covered by an old ordinance in Mankato, Minnesota. It's illegal to drive a bright red car within the limits of the community.

A female who is unmarried and under twenty-one years old is prohibited from wearing a corset in Maryville, Missouri. Local lawmakers felt that "the privilege of admiring the curvaceous unencumbered body of a young woman should not be denied to the normal red-blooded American male."

A bill purporting to be the answer to nasty spells of cold weather was introduced in the Ohio legislature. Under this law, January and February were to be abolished. Their days were to be transferred to the months of June, July, and August. Explained the Maumee, Ohio, legislator who brought up the bill:

57

"By eliminating the coldest days of the year and increasing the number of warm summer days, we could cut our energy needs by approximately one-third."

A number of states, incredibly enough, have passed laws actually allowing them to charge a sales tax on illegal drug sales. In Minnesota, for example, a law requires illicit drug dealers to put state excise stamps on all their cocaine, heroin, marijuana, or other illegal merchandise.

People who go to church in Storm Lake, Iowa, don't tend to hang around for long after the service is over. Why? Because an ordinance prohibits "loafing around a church."

Cream puffs once caught the wrath of the people who make the laws in Hillsboro, Ohio. The making and selling of cream puffs was banished in the community. Why such a strange law? Because these bakery delicacies were deemed to be "against the pure food laws."

Illinois is one of the first states where lawmakers made it against the law to speak English. "American" became the official state language because of a 1919 statute.

"Old maids, widows, and cautious women," according to an old law in Michigan, are allowed or even encouraged to check under their beds for a strange man. Doing this on a regular basis, says the law, "is not evidence of any mental deficiency."

An old piece of loony legislation in Indianapolis bans anyone from sending flowers to a person who is incarcerated in the city jail. This law, aptly enough, was called the "Anti-Jailbird-Flower-Senders-Ordinance."

Don't drink any beer in Missouri! You may not like the taste. The legislature came out with a strict law that specified all of the ingredients to be used in the correct brewing of beer. Unfortunately, the bright legislators who wrote the bill left out water!

Kids will have to be a little more careful around Webster City, Iowa. Bike riding is okay, but a local ordinance bans the riding of a bicycle with no wheels!

Ohio legislators must take their horses and their physicians quite seriously. It's illegal in Ohio to call a medical doctor a horse doctor, even in jest. So strict is this law that people are even prohibited from so calling a veterinarian who really *is* a horse doctor.

There's a strange piece of legislation regarding automobiles and horses in Milwaukee. The old law says: "No automobile may remain parked for over two hours unless it is hitched to a horse."

Here's another one for presidential hopefuls during election years. Minnesota voters may still be banned from using voting machines. Why? Because the Minnesota constitution once required that all elections be "by ballot." This clause was written long before voting machines were even invented. The Minnesota constitution is so crusted with age that it refers to "British possessions" in the clause fixing the state boundaries!

Carbondale, Illinois, residents have some protection against pushy landlords. A landlord is prohibited from evicting a tenant by shooting in his direction "with a loaded revolver." Must be okay to fire at a tenant with a shotgun, since the law mentioned only a revolver.

Children are allowed to play marbles for fun in Big Rapids, Michigan. But they can't play marbles "for keeps," says the law, "because they might grow up to be gamblers."

There aren't many spittoons left in Fort Wayne anymore. But an old ordinance governing the proper use of spittoons is still around today. Any person "missing a spittoon while spitting tobacco juice from any angle," is violating the law. Such action always brings a fine.

Tired of riding next to smelly people when taking a bus? Then move to Duluth. Any person who is unbathed, one who is wearing filthy clothing, or an individual who has strong body odor, can, by law, be tossed off city buses or other modes of public transportation.

Women in St. Louis must be extremely careful when going shopping for clothing. According to a local ordinance, a woman must purchase one dress for every six she tries on in any one store.

A person can eat cheese by itself anytime in Wisconsin. But one can never feast on apple pie by itself, without its cheese topping. The law says that apple pie cannot be served or eaten without a slice of cheese on top anywhere in the state.

Baseball players aren't highly thought of in Portsmouth, Ohio. An old ordinance says that these fellows rank right up there with "vagrants, hooligans, thieves, and other suspicious characters."

Citizens in Chambersburg, Illinois, have no problem when wanting to sport a mustache or sideburns. But "whiskers" can create a serious predicament—an old ordinance prohibits their growth.

Madison, Wisconsin, clears its streets and sidewalks relatively early with a curfew. The only thing allowed on the streets after 8:00 P.M. are "baby buggies and three-wheel vehicles with rubber tires."

No one can whistle at a female as she passes on the street in East Lansing, Michigan. This town has two ordinances that state loud noises and certain kinds of "voice motions or actions" may be considered to be offensive. A man who whistles at a woman can be charged with "offensive whistling" and with violating the local noise law. A $25 fine is given the whistler for violating the city noise limit. The charge of "offensive whistling" can bring a ninety-day jail term and a $100 fine.

Legislators in Iowa passed legislation to classify the Kansas state flower, the sunflower, "a noxious weed." Kansas legislators, as could be expected, were offended. They retaliated by classifying Iowa's state bird, the eastern goldfinch, "a public nuisance."

As silly as this may sound, it's against the law in Ohio for a boy to dig up and sell fishing worms in his own front yard. Nor can he catch and sell crayfish for bait. The state of Ohio actually requires that a child have a special permit, no matter how few worms or crayfish he is selling, or where he is selling them.

Illinois has an interesting statute on the books, one other states might like to consider adopting. Every able-bodied man between the ages of twenty-one and fifty, is required to donate two days each year to street repair work.

How a person walks on the streets of Willow Springs, Missouri, is carefully covered by a bit of loony legalese. It's illegal for a man to stroll around town while carrying one or both shoes in his hands or pockets. And a woman can't carry her shoes in a purse or a handbag.

> "A person assaulted and lynched by a mob may recover, from the county in which such assault is made, a sum not to exceed five hundred dollars." (Ohio statute)

7

Gulf Coast States' Laws

Not even George Washington's birthday is sanctified as a state holiday by constitutional fiat in Louisiana. But the birthday of Huey Long is recognized as such! Article XIX of the 63,000-word Louisiana constitution provides: "August 30, the birthday of Honorable Huey P. Long, now deceased, late governor of Louisiana, shall be and forever remain a legal holiday in this state."

Be extremely careful when driving anywhere around Lakeland, Florida. According to the law: "The operator of any motor vehicle is prohibited from allowing said vehicle to stand still on any street, road, or highway unless said vehicle is fastened down substantially."

No mortician who practices in Alabama is allowed to use "profane, indecent, or obscene language in the presence of a human dead body." An Alabama mortician who is heard doing this will lose his license! And any citizen who swears and curses while paying a visit to a funeral home, while a funeral is in progress, will be fined and jailed.

One small southern community wanted to warn drivers fairly by publicizing their local speed law. A highly visible sign was posted at the edge of Durant, Mississippi: "20 Miles an Hour or $19.90."

"No male person walking the streets, or lazily lounging on a street corner," declares the loony law in Natchitoches, Louisiana, "can lawfully wink at any unchaperoned female person, married or unmarried, unless he is already acquainted with said female person."

Palm Beach, Florida, has a unique law that makes it illegal to jog while topless. The law was specifically aimed at shirtless men, because, as one city councilman said: "There's nothing attractive about a hairy chest, dripping with perspiration. The residents of our city shouldn't be forced to look at such a sight."

Some places in this country simply do not condone romance and outward shows of affection. An old 1930 law in Phenix City, Alabama, prohibits a man from holding hands with a woman while walking down any street in the community.

The good old days must have been nice in some parts of Mississippi for drivers who liked to speed. Here's the law in one county: "All citizens traveling on the roads and highways in the County of Humphreys, State of Mississippi, will be limited to a speed of no more than 11 miles an hour. Shall there be no law officer visible in the distance, a driver is then allowed to make whatever speed he is able."

Residents of Baton Rouge, Louisiana, will think twice about complaining when their streets are in need of repairs. Any person who gripes about the poor condition of the street in front of his house may find himself in trouble. The complainer can be forced to repair the street himself.

In Wauchula, Florida, the city council passed a "No Knockers Ordinance." A spokesman explained: "The law was passed as a means of stopping dissatisfied citizens from continually knocking the city whenever they happened to disagree with decisions made by the council. It has absolutely nothing whatsoever to do with 'knockers' of the other kind."

Be careful when calling someone a name in Alabama. It's against the law to yell "Skunk" at another person.

And you can call someone Adolf, or you can call someone Hitler, but it's illegal to call anyone Adolf Hitler.

Mississippi has a strange piece of loony legislation concerning a particular piece of well-known music. A person can be fined and jailed for simply playing the "Missouri Waltz" on a piano!

Everyone strolling down the street is required to do something unusual in Key West, Florida. What? They must stop whatever they may be doing and "stand perfectly still when the clock strikes six."

Anyone who is thinking how much fun it would be to molest a skunk ape will have a serious problem in Florida. It's illegal there for any person to molest or otherwise attack a skunk ape so long as the beast is minding its own business. What is a skunk ape? Florida's homegrown version of the Abominable Snowman or Bigfoot!

Streetcars in Birmingham, Alabama, must have been rough-riding son-of-a-guns in the past. Things got so bad in fact that this strange law was passed to help alleviate the situation: "All streetcar lines . . . are prohibited from using flat wheels on their cars."

67

The cost of living for bald men in Louisiana is probably lower than in any other state in the nation. Why? Because legislation was actually passed regulating the cost of haircuts for bald men. There is a twenty-five-cent ceiling on such haircuts!

Snoring is even regulated in some parts of the Orange Juice State. For example, in Milton, Florida, no man "can snore in his own home, no matter how harmonious his snoring may sound, unless all doors and windows are tightly closed."

No man in Brookhaven, Mississippi, is allowed to attend a church function while wearing a "fake mustache." Why such a ridiculous law? Because any person so doing might disrupt the proceedings and "cause unbecoming laughter."

Anyone who owns or manages a store or other business in Meridian, Mississippi, is banned from telling customers about other customers who owe them money. Nor can shopkeepers reveal how much a customer spends on groceries, or what kind of groceries they purchase.

Kids won't have such a great time in Coffeeville, Mississippi. Local politicos took it upon themselves to outlaw marble playing, jacks, or pitching pennies anywhere in the business district of the community.

Florida has an old law that's apparently an attempt to clarify a fine point in the romantic realm—it isn't a crime for a man to try and pick up a woman as she strolls down a street. Why isn't such an action a crime? Because said the legislation: "It is a general tendency of men who see a pretty girl walking along the street to try and get acquainted."

Beer has been a fermenting issue in Alabama for years. Barbour County apparently solved the problem with special legislation. No one is allowed to sell, transport, or have in their home anything that "tastes like beer, smells like beer, or even looks like beer."

As one might expect from the land of southern gentlemen and hospitality, some old laws even follow a predictable pattern. Some years ago, Alabama lawmakers came up with a law giving "fat women" more time than the usual person would need for boarding a train. Such a woman, said the law, was also entitled to more time for getting off a train.

The Good Humor Man and other ice cream peddlers can't "cry or holler in a loud voice" as they call out their wares while passing through a neighborhood in

Lake Charles, Louisiana. Nor can they use anything more than a "soft chime" to attract the attention of potential customers.

Nothing like having equal rights for women in Alabama. A bill was finally passed in the state legislature concerning women and coal mines. Females over the age of eighteen are now allowed to work in Alabama coal mines!

Merchants in Gulfport, Mississippi, must be careful how they induce customers to come into their stores. Store owners can't "grab, hit, strike, kick, drag, or pull" a person off the street in order to make a sale.

The speed of a train in Tallahassee, Florida, is nicely covered by a city ordinance. According to this law, no train "is permitted to run through the city at a speed faster than an ordinary citizen can walk."

Railroad cars, when they are seen to be standing still in Andalusia, Alabama, "must be properly chained together." No railroad box cars can be left on a siding "unless they are properly chained."

It's against the law in Philadelphia, Mississippi, for any man, woman, or child to engage in a barking contest with a dog. To do so can bring a $10 fine for "insulting public behavior."

Pity the poor Florida driver! According to one old law, "When a motorist sights a horse and buggy approaching on the road ahead, he must pull over, park, and cover his car. A heavy piece of canvas is best for this purpose. The horse must be allowed to pass undisturbed. Should the horse become skittish, the motorist must dismantle his vehicle in its entirety. Each piece must be hidden under or behind some bushes or trees."

Mississippi, widely known as a teetotaling state since 1908, operates under a funny old law. The state collects taxes on the liquor consumed in Mississippi, even though liquor is illegal! This is done under a "black market" law, which provides for a 10 percent tax on "any personal property the sale of which is prohibited." Mississippi does a thriving business in bootleg booze. So big is this enterprise that it easily supports a tax collector who makes three times as much salary as does the governor, and it keeps the fellow three times as busy.

An old ordinance in Tallulah, Louisiana, prohibits local citizens from walking around the rear of a mule without first speaking to the animal. If the mule kicks,

71

the person kicked is charged with "contributory negligence"!

Fruit peddlers or stores in Tallapoosa County, Alabama, have to be careful how they prepare their apples for sale. No one is allowed to coat apples with high-gloss varnish in order to better bring out their beauty.

There are a lot of unusual things the law in Mississippi says people can't do. A strange one deals with cotton—it can't be bought or sold after sundown or before sunup.

Alligators are well looked after in Leesburg, Florida. An ordinance prohibits anyone from "molesting" one of these creatures.

> "Every citizen has the right to shoot to kill if necessary when escorting a woman home from a quilting party and another man interferes and threatens to shoot him." (Mississippi common law)

8

Laws in the Northwest

It's still unlawful in Wyoming for the driver of a stagecoach to leave his horses unattended, no matter how short a time. Such a careless driver can be fined for a first offense, put in jail for a second.

An old ordinance in Burley, Idaho, actually regulates the size of a box of candy a fellow can bestow upon his fiancée after they get engaged. Such sweets must never weigh less than fifty pounds!

Whatever could poor little goldfish have done to draw the ire of the lawmakers in Seattle? Here's the weird ordinance: "It is unlawful to carry a goldfish on public transportation unless that goldfish is lying down."

Sleeping and driving simply don't mix in Watertown, South Dakota. One old ordinance requires the police to pull drivers over when they are seen to be asleep holding the reins while driving a horse and buggy!

The driver is then to be given a ticket. This same law can be applied to the drivers of automobiles.

Lawmakers in Minot, North Dakota, came up with an ordinance to help parents avoid any liability for their children's mischief. All the father and mother had to do was post a sign conspicuously on the kid. The sign had to have a white background with eight-inch red letters saying, BEWARE OF WILD CHILD.

Even certain puppets are carefully covered by law in the community of Salmon, Idaho. The only way a Punch-and-Judy puppet show can be presented in Salmon is if the puppets "wear distinctively American clothes."

Incredibly enough, some communities even have laws that actually regulate certain illegal activities. For example, a burglar has to be careful when in Okanogah, Washington. An ordinance specifies that he "can steal only after dark."

What happens when an angry wife berates her husband in public anywhere within the limits of Plentywood, Montana? If her activities draw a crowd of spectators, says an ordinance, her husband can be fined! Why? Because, says the law, a man is responsible for his spouse's behavior. The same kind of law is found in Dixie, Idaho.

Some animals can have all the privacy they want in Alaska. The legislature passed a law making it illegal for anyone flying over in an airplane to look down on a moose. No one in Alaska seems to know how this strange legislation can possibly be enforced, or even why it should be.

A special law in Cheyenne, Wyoming, covers the weight of the attire worn by a dancer as she performs in any establishment where beer or liquor is served. The performer must always be found wearing clothing weighing "a minimum of three pounds, eight ounces."

Most people believe it would be easier to fish with a fishing rod, line, hook, and bait. Evidently this isn't the case in Hoover, South Dakota. Lawmakers there took it upon themselves to pass a law prohibiting anyone from "fishing with a kerosene lantern."

People in one Idaho community must always appear to be happy when seen in public places. Rexburg retains an old ordinance prohibiting local citizens from walking down the street while "looking gloomy."

Popping a horse with a peashooter has been banned within the limits of Dickinson, North Dakota. Anyone using a peashooter for this purpose is guilty of a misdemeanor.

It's against the law for any city or town in the state of Washington to furnish residents with off-street parking. Nor can local politicians set the working hours at City Hall. Even engaging in slum clearance is illegal! The legislature must first be petitioned for permission to do all of these things and more.

Laramie, Wyoming, is not a good place for house-to-house salesmen to work. A salesman must have an invitation before going up to a house and trying to make a sale.

An assemblyman from Anchorage, Alaska, introduced a bill prohibiting "flatulence, crepitation, gaseous emission, and miasmic effluence." This legislative legalese would make breaking wind in public a misdemeanor. And such an action would be punishable with a $100 fine!

Some people will steal anything—but an outhouse? Yes! Outhouse stealing was so prevalent in some parts of North Dakota that special laws had to be passed. In Grafton, for example, a person who gets caught

76

stealing an outhouse will be given a $50 fine for a first offense.

People in Lidgerwood, North Dakota, for example, must be careful when they decide to snooze in a neighbor's outhouse. It's against the law to use someone else's outhouse as a place to catch a catnap—unless you have first gotten their permission.

However, in little Bowbells, North Dakota, a catnap is okay while making use of an outhouse. But spending the night sleeping in one is taboo.

Movies are loads of fun to many people in Bend, Oregon. But an ordinance determines when horror flicks can and can't be seen. According to the law, horror films can be shown in a local theater only on Monday, Tuesday, and Wednesday.

Senior citizens will have to stay on their feet in Sand Point, Idaho. According to the law, any person over the age of eighty-eight is banned from riding a motorcycle. Keep on truckin' . . . but do it on foot.

Don't expect to be treated with respect in Bellingham, Washington, if you walk up to a bar and order a bottle of beer. It's against the law in this part of the Ever-

77

green State for anyone to drink beer while standing up in a bar.

Beware if you are ever around horses in Ashland, Oregon. No man is allowed to whistle loudly in public places if a horse happens to be in the vicinity. Why? Because city fathers have allowed that horses might be frightened by the whistling sounds you emit. Strangely enough, a woman can whistle any time she wishes under the same circumstances. Females aren't mentioned anywhere in this old piece of loony legalese.

Physicians who practice in Kalispell, Montana, seem to have a special responsibility regarding all of the local kids. An unusual piece of loony legislation says a child must have a doctor's permission in order to buy a lollipop or a candy bar while church services are in session.

South Dakota is rough on theater managers. No movie can be shown which contains scenes depicting "illicit lovemaking or an illicit love relationship." Nor can a movie be shown with any "infidelity segments." And last, films are banned from South Dakota theaters that "contain murder scenes, or that have a murder plot."

Married women must be careful when they start their spring cleaning in Ketchikan, Alaska. No furniture can be moved around a room without the permission of the husband.

Like a good game of cards? Well, be extremely cautious in Donnelly, Idaho. An antiquated city ordinance prohibits anyone from playing cards on a riverbank while waiting for the fish to start biting.

A driver going through Glasgow, Montana, isn't allowed to honk his horn at a horse and buggy when pulling up from behind. Nor can he pass a horse-drawn carriage on the road without first stopping the automobile and politely asking permission of the carriage driver.

Baker City, Oregon, has a strange law regarding the bathing of babies. No adult can legally put two babies in a tub and then proceed to bathe them at the same time. Apparently three or four babies can take a bath together, since this ordinance specifically mentions only two.

People living in Lander, Wyoming, may find they have a serious problem when cold weather sets in. A local ordinance prohibits children from taking a bath during the winter. Adults, per this law, are allowed

79

one bath per month. Children under fourteen years old can have none!

There's an odd piece of loony legalese governing hunters and fishermen in Mandaree, North Dakota. An old law prohibits any man in the community from going hunting or fishing unless he first gets written permission from his wife. To get caught hunting or fishing without a signed note could bring a fine and some time in jail.

Lewistown, Montana, might really be a great place to live for nonsmokers. An ordinance prohibits citizens from smoking cigarettes, a pipe, or "segar" in any public building, a restaurant, or on any street, road, or highway.

Fishermen would certainly enjoy living around Kodiak, Alaska. An old piece of loony legislation stops local citizens from "sticking out a tongue," or otherwise "making mockery" of a person who has just caught a small fish.

Klamath Falls, Oregon, has an odd ordinance governing how a kid may act when out in public. It's against the law for a boy to walk around with his hands stuck in his pockets on Sunday. And it's also illegal for a child to blow a whistle and embarrass his parents during church services.

The state of Washington once found a use for a small part of its dog population. According to one old law, each and every train running in Washington must have a dog sitting on the cowcatcher in front of a steam engine.

Stay away from rugged Rawlins, Wyoming, if you happen to own an ugly dog. This community has a strange law on the books that makes it illegal to walk an ugly dog down any public thoroughfare. Who determines which dogs are ugly? No one really knows. A small fine can be imposed on anyone who violates this silly ordinance.

No horse can be given a plug of chewing tobacco within the boundaries of Williston, North Dakota. A special law was long ago passed to prohibit all such dire activities. To give a horse a chew could bring a fine and jail time. But since the law makes no mention of them, snuff, a cigarette, or even a cigar would be legal to give a horse.

No child should be seen spitting on the ground within sight of other people on the Sabbath anywhere in Winner, South Dakota. They have a special ordinance governing this type of activity. And children are also prohibited from loudly burping on Sunday while walking down the street.

Want to raise beef cattle but find you have no room for grazing your herd? You'll be in deep trouble if you try to use a cemetery within the boundaries of Eugene, Oregon. It's illegal to graze cattle in such a place.

If you happen to be out after dark in Miles City, Montana, expect to experience the unusual. Miles City has banned all horses from the city streets after the sun has gone down. But this old law has a loophole: a person is allowed to ride a horse at night if a bright red light is first securely tied to the horse's tail.

Gillette, Wyoming, doesn't allow the shooting of rats and other small rodents while walking, riding a horse, or driving an automobile through the streets of the community. The penalty for rat hunting? A dose of castor oil. And this penalty is to be forcibly administered, if necessary, by the citizen who witnessed the illegal shooting activity.

There's an old Sunday flying law in Washburn, North Dakota. No one is allowed to fly a plane over the community on Sunday between 11:00 A.M. and 1:00

82

P.M. Nor can a plane land or take off during this same time period.

Going out to eat while visiting the state of Washington? You'll find it especially interesting to order a meal when visiting Asotin County. An ordinance requires that menus in every restaurant have to be written "in the American language."

"No citizens shall allow their turkeys, chickens, cattle, horses, lions, or tigers to be led by chains along a street in this community." (Grangeville, Idaho, ordinance)

9

Western Laws

Wife beating legal in San Francisco in 1849? Yes! Such an activity was generally overlooked by the court. If a wife beater was prosecuted, it wasn't for the beating itself but rather for "disturbing the peace." One judge heard a case involving a rough-and-tumble miner who had noisily spanked his wife, thereby interrupting the peace and quiet of his neighbors. After levying a $10 fine, His Honor declared: "It is no great harm to whip some wives, provided the public are not disturbed by the operation."

"A motorist must send up red warning rockets and Roman candles at night when approaching a horse," says an old Nebraska statute. "He must also throw a camouflage tarpaulin over his car to conceal it from the horse. If this does not calm the animal, the motorist must dismantle his auto and hide the parts in the grass."

Here's a lulu from Sparks, Nevada: "A citizen is forbidden to drive a donkey along Main Street in August without a straw hat being worn." The law is unclear as to who has to wear the straw hat—the jackass or the driver!

Even how fast steers and other livestock may or may not move is covered by a loony law in Durango, Colorado. Cattle are prohibited from moving slower than 2.5 miles per hour when on a road or a highway.

Basset hounds have specific restrictions on their howling and barking according to the law in Los Osos, California. Bassets are prohibited from barking or howling more than once every hour. They are banned from barking or howling for more than two minutes at any one time. And they can *never* bark or howl between 8:00 P.M. and 8:00 A.M.

The law in Lincoln, Nebraska, covers an unusual aspect of burglary: "Burglars are prohibited from entering or leaving the scene of a crime by the front door."

Utah apparently knows how to handle drunks. Their law is quite specific: "Intoxicated persons are prohibited from operating a vehicle on any public highway or street, except for a wheelbarrow."

Wouldn't this stir up a hornet's nest with the local politicians in Hollywood, California, if someone owned enough sheep? A sheep drive down the streets of Hollywood isn't illegal! It's the number of sheep in the drive that counts. An old ordinance prohibits the driving of "more than 2,000 sheep through the city of Hollywood at one time."

Sleeping in motels and rooming houses in Kansas may not be all that bad. The mattresses may be filled with goose feathers. Why? Because by Kansas law, mattresses made of "moss, sea grass, or excelsior" are forbidden.

Cedar City, Utah, has at one time or another had a variety of unusual clothing laws directed at women. High buckle shoes, for instance, are the only kind to be seen on a woman's feet when she goes shopping or does anything else in public. Another law bans women from attending church while attired in house shoes or slippers.

An old law in Leadville, Colorado, clearly describes how a bull has to be equipped while walking on a highway. Each bull must wear a bell, a whistle or a horn, a headlight, and a tail light.

It's illegal in California to eat or even serve other people dog meat. The same statute protects cats as well. It seems some Vietnamese refugees in San Francisco and other areas of the state have been trapping and hunting dogs and cats for the sole purpose of cooking and eating them!

All teaching applicants in Nevada must swear they have never "participated in a duel, as a principal or a second." Anyone ever involved in a duel is prohibited from teaching in the Nevada school system.

Women in Beatrice, Nebraska, sometimes enjoy baking and cooking as a method of pleasing their men. These homemakers bake apple, peach, berry, and just about any other kind of pie. But according to the law in Beatrice, no one can make and bake a mince pie under any circumstances!

Don't go to Riverside, California, if you like to walk to work and carry your lunch. No one in this town is allowed to carry a lunch pail or a lunch box on any street within the limits of the community.

People who live in Tremonton, Utah, must have an ongoing problem with mice. The law bans citizens from setting mousetraps anywhere in a house, in a barn, and in the yard around the house.

According to the law in Salina, Kansas, railroad bums, or those better known as hoboes, aren't allowed to sleep in a moving boxcar. There is one notable exception to this law. A hobo can nap in a boxcar anytime he chooses if he first has a consultation with the railroad's president!

A woman can normally propose to a man anytime she wishes in Elko, Nevada. But she had better not try this during leap year! The law says she'll be "guilty of misconduct and inappropriate behavior."

Santa Monica, California, may be unusually sensitive to the problems of renters. For example, if the plastic covers on electrical outlets happen to be cracked, a renter may be entitled to a $25-a-month rent reduction. Should a garbage disposal unit break down on a Friday night and not be repaired until the following Monday, a rent reduction of $35 a month may be obtained.

Snuff is readily available around Columbus, Nebraska. But according to a local ordinance, a man must stand a "full arm's length away from the seller" when purchasing a can of snuff for his personal use.

Many things have changed since the era of Charles Dickens and debtor's prisons. However, the thinking of lawmakers in Salt Lake City may be Dickensian. These people passed an ordinance to take care of tenants who don't pay their rent. They'll be sent to cool their feet in a jail cell. Anyone living in Salt Lake City who misses one rent payment is subject to criminal prosecution.

Attorneys must not be highly thought of, or much in demand, around Emporia, Kansas. An odd local ordinance allows "any voter of good character to practice law in any courtroom in the city of Emporia."

Clocks are apparently an important part of daily life in Visalia, California. An ordinance allows any businessperson to hang a clock over a sidewalk, with a certain specific condition: the clock must keep correct time!

Move over, folks, when a fireman approaches you on the sidewalk. The law in Hiawatha, Kansas, always gives the right of way to the fireman. And it matters not if the fire fighter is coming from, or going to, work.

Dunkin' Donuts stores in many sections of the country sell doughnut holes by the dozen. Yet in Chadron, Nebraska, it's against the law for anyone to sell these taste tempters to the customers of a bakery.

Leave it to those California legislators! They must have had nothing better to do with their time, so they spent it coming up with a loony statute prohibiting the use of dirty underwear for housecleaning rags.

It's against the law in Honolulu for a fellow to drop his swim trunks and moon a police car while in a moving vehicle on Kalakaua Avenue on the way to Waikiki Beach. A man who exposes his bared rear in this manner can get up to ten days in jail and a $250 fine. Evidently this ordinance doesn't cover women who might try mooning police officers under identical circumstances.

People out joyriding in an automobile around Montrose, Colorado, can be stopped and apprehended by the police if their bare feet are seen hanging out the window. The law says absolutely nothing about feet with shoes on them!

Nebraska's Lancaster County came up with a great way to control their pet population. They passed an ordinance requiring mating permits for all dogs and cats. Such permits, naturally, have a price tag—in this case a $3 fee. One county supervisor offered this philosophical tidbit: "I can't think of any way to communicate the idea to the dog or cat." No kidding! A question: who is expected to pay for this permit, the pet owner or the pet?

A man or a woman in Provo, Utah, can sit on a park bench next to a member of the opposite sex and hold a conversation. But the person will be arrested if he or she sits closer than eight inches. This eight-inch space requirement holds true even if the couple sitting together happens to be married.

A most unusual eating law can be found in Redding, California. The loony legalese reads: "Shoes are required to eat in any restaurant or other place serving food to the public." How such an ordinance could ever be enforced is highly questionable. After all, exactly how much can a pair of shoes eat? And what should they eat?

Any jackass who breaks out of its stall or through a fence is held responsible by the law in Longmont, Colorado. An escaping jackass is required to pay for all damages he may have caused. This kind of law might just scare a whole lot of politicians!

The politicians who run Fallon, Nevada, may not know about this next law. Some of them even smoke cigarettes while public meetings are in progress. That's okay—if the cigarettes are store bought! But an old law makes it a misdemeanor to roll your own cigarettes and smoke them during public meetings. Such a smoker can get a $500 fine!

91

Every public vehicle in San Francisco—bus, trolley, cable car, police cruiser, taxicab, etc.—must be outfitted with a spittoon. City officials can actually be prosecuted for not making certain there's a spittoon in each and every vehicle used by the public or used in the public's behalf.

Pipe smokers will have to beware while in Burlington, Colorado. People who puff on cigars and cigarettes have no particular restrictions on them. But pipe smokers—alas, that's a different story entirely. No one is ever permitted to smoke a pipe on any city street after the sun sets.

Bees could be a serious problem in Chanute, Kansas. Driving a car with "bees in your bonnet" is forbidden by law. The ordinance doesn't specify whether real live bees are meant, or decorative bees, but it's still the law!

Watch out, fellows, if you're taking a young woman out on the town in Alamosa, Colorado. You'll have to be careful where you take her for a good time—especially if she loves dancing. A local ordinance prohibits a man from escorting a woman under the age of twenty-one to a dance.

Native Americans in Cima, California, were never welcome in the community except under specific guidelines. An old law reads: "No Indians are allowed in town except when they are dressed in white man's clothing."

Sugarville, Utah, has outlawed voters from taking pictures of political candidates on the Sabbath. Neither adults nor children are allowed to bother a politician while he or she is trying to catch a short nap, or is obviously trying to relax for a few minutes.

Be careful when going to a baseball, basketball, or football game in Hyannis, Nebraska. A local ordinance prohibits spectators from listening to a radio while a ball game or other sporting event is in progress.

"When two trains approach each other at a crossing, they shall both come to a full stop, and neither shall start up until the other has gone." (Kansas statute)

II

More Laughable Laws

10

A Special Selection of Blue-Nosed Blue Laws

The year was 1875, and the ice cream soda was about a year old and fast gaining in popularity. However, in Evanston, Illinois, the elders of the Methodist church were taking a very dim view of this ice cream treat. Some of these church leaders believed that "soda water" (carbonated water) was a "mite intoxicating." Community leaders were pressured to vote to forbid the selling and serving of ice cream sodas on Sundays—on the premise that they were a corrupting influence on all.

The town was shocked at the ban on ice cream sodas. And in W. C. Garwood's Drug Store, it was worse than shocking! It hurt sales at the soda fountain, which was the favorite gathering place of youngsters, families and Sunday-strolling sweethearts.

To get around the local law, an enterprising fountain clerk started to serve scoops of ice cream, dribbled over with thick syrup, minus the "mite intoxicating" soda water. The soda-less sodas became the "Sunday sodas," all quite legal in every way. However, they became so popular that customers began asking for "Sundays" all through the week.

The church elders were indignant at having been outwitted. In an attempt to have the last word, they raised objections to the fact that the dish was named after the Sabbath. Again ingenuity stepped in—and the spelling was altered to *sundae*.

They're obsolete, confusing, and frequently ridiculous. But laws restricting Sunday fun and trade and travel still make criminals out of many otherwise law-abiding citizens. For example, a thirsty kid in Nooseneck, Rhode Island, can't buy any kind of a soft drink or an ice cream soda on the Sabbath without first getting a note from his mother.

Here's another great blue law to consider: No child can expect to be able to roller-skate into a store and order any kind of a soft drink. It's illegal for a child to buy or drink a soda while on roller skates in any public establishment on the Sabbath in Danbury, Connecticut.

Thousands of Americans have run into trouble with the law for committing the following "offenses":

Painting the outside of a house in Roanoke Rapids, Virginia; delivering two quarts of fresh milk in Bristol, Vermont; and selling six mousetraps in Natchez, Mississippi.

Serious legal problems have erupted for simply playing a game of baseball before lunch in Trinidad, Colorado; working on an automobile in Prineville, Oregon; trimming a couple of choice T-bone steaks in Millville, New Jersey; and selling Limburger cheese in Houston, Texas.

It's also against the law in Williamston, North Carolina, to offer gum or candy to a woman in church in order to get her attention. To do so can bring a fine of $1.50 and a day in jail. And candy and ice cream lovers should avoid Snowville, New Hampshire. A local ordinance bans buying or eating candy on Sunday.

All of the above lawbreakers have one thing in common: they did what they did—and were caught in the act—on a Sunday. At the root of all the trouble are America's countless (and often controversial) "blue laws," the term most commonly applied to ordinances and statutes that prohibit certain kinds of Sunday activities. Religious in origin, many of these blue laws date back to the Puritanical rules of behavior that flourished in the New England colonies. In 1781 the Reverend Samuel A. Peters called them "blue laws" in his *General History of Connecticut*, but the term wasn't his innovation. In 1648, Puritan leaders in Connecticut had come up with a number of restrictive Sabbath-related laws, had them bound between blue covers, and called them blue laws.

Colonial blue laws originally forbade "immoral" behavior on all days of the week. This included smoking tobacco, drinking liquor, watching or indulging in certain amusements. Colonists were directed "to avoid any frivolity." "Lusty young men" in the colonies were sternly rebuked for wanting "to pitch ye barr, and play at stoole ball and such like sports."

Today's blue laws generally mean laws restricting business, sporting events, and other things on Sunday. Many of these laws draw their strength from the Bible's Book of Exodus, describing how God gave the Ten Commandments to Moses. The Scriptures read: "Remember the sabbath day, to keep it holy. Six days shalt thou labor, and do all thy work, but the seventh day is the sabbath in honor of the Lord thy God; on it thou shalt not do any work. . . ."

Many states and untold numbers of counties and municipalities still have blue laws aimed at curtailing

100

Sunday work, business, and play. These state and local laws vary widely, but they generally share this key sentence: "All labor on Sunday is prohibited, except works of necessity and charity."

Thus an increasingly large number of blue-law violations crop up as obsolete regulations clash with the demands of modern society. The law in New York State is a case in point. The following is permissible: before 10:00 A.M., food may be sold; after 1:00 P.M., beer; between 4:00 P.M. and 7:30 P.M., cooked and prepared food can be sold by delicatessens, bakeries, and grocery stores; in communities with less than 40,000 population, farm produce or fishing tackle may be sold from roadside stands all day on Sunday; all over the state, regardless of population, these items can be sold all day: restaurant meals, catered meals, bread, milk, ice, fruit, souvenirs, newspapers, gasoline, etc. But at no time can uncooked meats be sold, anywhere in the state.

The same pressures and business lobbies that caused the above exceptions to the law also modified Sunday restrictions on sporting events. In New York State the law reads: "All public sports . . . shows . . . and all noise disturbing the peace of the day are prohibited." The law goes on to state that any form of public sports or shows may be conducted on the first day of

101

the week after 2:00 P.M. Why the insistence on a 2:00 P.M. start? To permit spectators to attend Sunday church services.

Every now and then the police are enlisted to enforce the laws strictly. Suddenly there is a spate of weird, often ridiculous arrests. In Bucks County, Pennsylvania, for example, a justice of the peace tried to demonstrate how ludicrous blue laws sometimes are. On two Sundays in July, he ordered the arrests of 225 Sunday "lawbreakers." The justice of the peace even fined Pennsylvania Turnpike toll collectors, who were charged with doing illegal "worldly work" on Sunday.

Police suddenly began to enforce the Sunday closing law in Nashville, Tennessee. Many businesspeople were arrested. To make a point, Judge Andrew Doyle instructed the police to start enforcing local blue laws 100 percent or not at all. Doyle said: "The only thing you can do on Sunday is charity. Bring me every preacher that preaches on Sunday, every bus that runs on Sunday, every show that opens on Sunday. . . . We are going to close this town down."

In Pella, Iowa, the blue-law keepers once banned swimming on Sundays. Therefore a special referendum was authorized to decide whether Pella's children could swim on the Holy Day. It was decided they could! Thereafter, however, the ban was again placed in effect—and still is. Children often have been reported as Sunday "lawbreakers" for fishing and hunting, playing organized baseball and football (except where games were held to raise church funds), and going to the movies.

Movie theaters have undergone a long struggle to stay open on Sundays. In New York, a 1909 case first permitted movies to be shown on Sunday. But even today there are still states and cities that prohibit showing films on Sunday, or at least for part of the day. In 1953, for example, the Vermont legislature killed a bill that would have legalized Sunday movie matinees.

Here's an oldie from one Pennsylvania city: Try to stay away from New Castle if you'd like to be free to go fishing on Sunday and need lots of worms for bait. It's against the law for a person to dig more than twelve worms on any one Sunday to use for fishing bait.

Many blue-law offenses stem from the automobile age in which we live. There are specific laws covering car washing, repairing, and racing on Sunday in San Antonio and other cities throughout the United States.

103

The solution to the problem of selling cars on Sunday varies from state to state and even within states—used car lots are often open, new car showrooms closed.

A number of years ago a law was passed in Indiana prohibiting car sales on Sunday, but the courts declared it unconstitutional. The decision was later reversed.

In New Jersey, a highway service station was prosecuted for washing a car on Sunday. The case went to the State Supreme Court, which held that "offenders could not be convicted as disorderly persons."

Because they came into existence in this century, cars confuse local officials following the letter of laws written in bygone times. For example, a young New Yorker was working on his sports car near his home in the Bronx. A police officer gave the sports car owner a ticket for "working" on Sunday. When the case came to court, the judge dismissed the charges, ruling that by changing his spark plugs the car owner "was not disturbing the Sunday peace."

A case heard in a federal appeals court concerned a kosher market in Springfield, Massachusetts. The market and several of its customers contended that the Massachusetts Lord's Day Act, which forces

stores to close on Sunday, discriminated against Jew-
ish shoppers, whose Sabbath is Saturday, not Sunday.
The court ruled in favor of the kosher market, declar-
ing the Lord's Day Act void because it favored one
religion over another.

With all the furor over blue laws, it would seem that
the last thing needed are more of them. Yet this is
what happened in New Jersey a few years ago. A
referendum asked the voters whether they wished to
bar the Sunday sale of clothing, home and office
furnishings, appliances, and building materials. The
referendum prohibiting such sales passed in twelve of
the fifteen counties polled. As a result, Sunday shopping continued in some counties and not in others.

In the meantime, the blue-law pot boils merrily. In
Connecticut the law is so vague that a suburbanite
may be breaking it when he mows his lawn on Sunday. Maine law bans citizens from happily whistling
on the Sabbath—even if the person happens to be
whistling a hymn! And gum-chomping or candy-
eating adults as well as children can be penalized in
St. Johnsbury, Vermont, should they make chewing
or slurping noises while attending a church service.

Even the popular hamburger has come under fire in
some areas of the country. No one in Roundup,

105

Montana, is allowed to buy, sell, or eat hamburgers on the Sabbath. And are you a man or a woman who happens to like wearing shorts on the Sabbath? If so, then don't get caught in public while astride a horse in Spearfish, South Dakota. It's a violation of the local blue laws for a male or female to be seen wearing shorts on the back of a horse on a Sunday.

Nor can Rice Krispies, Cheerios, or corn flakes be sold on Sunday anywhere in Logan, West Virginia. And guys and gals should look out when on a date in Valdosta, Georgia. This city has outlawed what they call "unseeming displays of affection on the Sabbath."

Restaurants in Kansas are prohibited from serving cherry pie with ice cream on the Sabbath. But cherry pie or ice cream *by itself* can be served. People in Kansas can eat just about anything they wish, from hamburgers to steaks and bacon to pork roast on Sunday. But for some absurd reason, Kansas legislators felt they had to pass a law to somehow protect the citizenry from eating snakes, tarantulas, scorpions, lizards, and centipedes.

Regular milk may be sold on Sunday in Clinton, Missouri, but the sale of buttermilk is banned. And ministers in Ashland, Wisconsin, are prohibited from purchasing or eating raw onions on the Sabbath.

106

Sunday blue laws are enforced only when society wants them to be enforced. Run a red light and you'll get a summons; open your grocery store on Sunday and you may or may not be arrested—depending on the temper of the community. But more and more, courts across the country are frowning on overeager cops and legislators—which means that perhaps in the near future all blue laws may simply fade away.

> "Any person who displays, handles, or uses any kind of reptile in connection with any religious service or gathering shall be fined not less than fifty dollars nor more than one hundred dollars." (Kentucky statute)

11

Laughable Laws Regarding Politicians

North Carolina voters need to check with Senator Jesse Helms on this one! According to the law, there's no need for a politician in the Tar Heel State to try to induce certain citizens to get on his or her bandwagon. Any North Carolina man who has been convicted of wife beating isn't allowed to cast his vote in an election.

Tennessee's constitution was amended five times since 1953. One provision of the original document actually barred ministers of the Gospel from running for and serving a term in the state legislature.

The law in the Bluegrass State protects voters from getting ticketed for speeding, running stop signs, or breaking any other driving law under certain circumstances. Here's the law as found in section 149 of the Kentucky constitution: "Voters, in all cases except treason, felony, breach or surety of the peace, or violation of the election laws, shall be privileged from arrest during their attendance at elections and while they are going to and returning therefrom."

Here's a law in Baltimore, Maryland, that might just apply to quite a number of politicians if it were to blossom out and be adopted in other areas of the nation. Should it, this law could create havoc in the halls of Congress and in state legislatures across the nation. The decree reads that "any services performed by a jackass must be recorded."

The state house of representatives in Austin, Texas, passed a capital punishment bill. The law requires "mandatory death sentences for murderers of firemen, prison guards, and police officers killed in the line of duty." One lawmaker wanted to add an amendment to include legislators. But another house member, deadly serious, responded: "This amendment is frivolous, because the people of Texas know that a member of the legislature is not worth killing."

Getting the attention of voters is the lifeblood of any good political campaign. But alas, running for public office in Oshkosh, Wisconsin, may be tough on candidates. A local ordinance prevents the playing of a fife and drum on any city street.

109

The Missouri legislature must be an extremely busy group of politicians. So overworked are these people that they actually took the time to consider a silly piece of legislation dealing with choosing an official watermelon inspector. The person selected for the job would be called, per the odd bill, "The Official Plugger, Muncher, and Taster of the State of Missouri."

The New Jersey constitution of 1844 was evidently designed to keep politicians constantly on the go. Each member of the Garden State assembly was compelled by law to run for election every year. This legality would certainly keep New Jersey politicians in a dither!

All meetings of public groups—mayoral, city council, meetings of the legislature, etc.—are required by statute in the Buckeye State to be open to the public. The Ohio General Assembly passed a special law to this effect! These same politicians then turned around and had the audacity to rule that the law they wrote and passed didn't apply to their own caucuses.

Only one kind of advertising circular is allowed on the streets of Montgomery, Alabama. A city ordinance says that only handbills used by politicians while running for office are allowed. These can be given to people or posted on telephone poles, in the windows of businesses, etc.

And the law in Guyman, Oklahoma, states that a politician isn't allowed to distribute handbills in front of any local school or church as a means of garnering votes.

Candidates who happen to be running for public office in Valentine, Nebraska, may have a difficult time getting to know the voters. Why? Because it's against the law in Valentine to "call, shout, or holler" at someone seen walking down any street in the community.

Tennessee for many years retained an odd kind of poll tax. Every citizen had to pay it before being allowed to vote. The tax consisted of a designated number of squirrel scalps, crow scalps, or wolf scalps. Perhaps Senator Al Gore or Jim Sasser should be consulted on this one.

The use of profanity in Rapid City, South Dakota, is prohibited under certain circumstances. No one is allowed to "curse or swear or use any sort of offensive language" while talking to the mayor or any other city officials.

111

And citizens in Missoula, Montana, must always be careful to show the proper respect to elected officials. An ordinance requires every man to lift his hat to the mayor as he passes on foot or drives by in an automobile.

The Lone Star State has an odd yet quite practical piece of legislation regarding a polling place. No Texan, per this law, is allowed to carry a spear or a sword with them when they go to cast a vote during an election.

Politics and politicians were quite different in days gone by. Candidates in Dotham, Alabama, are somewhat restricted as to how far they can go to attain political office. No politician, while campaigning, can engage in a duel with either another politician or a potential voter.

By federal law, no one can throw tomatoes or eggs, rotten or otherwise, at a member of Congress who is making a speech or campaigning for office. Assaulting a congressperson is a federal crime that carries a maximum sentence of one year in prison and a $5,000 fine.

Lucedale, Mississippi, certainly won't appeal much to horse lovers. This quiet little community has a rather

112

strange law on the books. It's illegal for any person to be found riding or sitting on a horse at a political rally.

Want to take your favorite horse to hear the candidates speak? Then beware of going to Denison, Iowa. An old law says that a voter can be charged with "willful negligence" for bringing a horse to a political rally.

Blythe, California, goes the other direction. No political candidate can ride a horse in a parade or along the streets of the community in order to attract the attention of potential voters.

In Wheatfield, Indiana, no woman can be seen wearing shorts and a halter or a bathing suit while attending a political rally. Every female must "suitably cover her body" before she can go and listen to a candidate who is running for office.

Elizabethtown, Kentucky, has a strange barefoot ordinance. No adult can stroll around barefoot at a political rally, or while a politician is making a speech.

A politician's wife in Dayville, Oregon, can water down hubby's bottle of alcoholic beverages. This can be done secretly in order to help stop the fellow from having one too many while campaigning. According

113

to this legislation, it's her *responsibility* to weaken his drinks!

Would you believe the following? There's actually a loony law in pretty little Holly Springs, Mississippi, prohibiting political candidates from entering a contest to catch a greased pig.

And Raleigh, North Carolina, won't let politicians participate in a certain rodeo event during a campaign. It's strictly illegal for any candidate for public office to rope a calf in an attempt to attract votes.

It's against the law in Colts Neck, New Jersey, for a man attending a political rally to kiss a woman, or a woman to kiss a man, within 300 feet of the speaker's platform.

Nor can politicians in Savannah, Tennessee, hum the "Star-Spangled Banner" while campaigning on the Sabbath.

Keep right on grinning while on the campaign trail if you happen to be in Las Animas, Colorado. It's illegal for a politician not to smile at any of the local citizenry—even if asked a question you don't like!

Nor can a political candidate in Rockland, Maine, make disparaging faces at children who are found to

114

be noisy and distracting during his or her campaign speech.

Enjoy playing chess? Well, be extremely cautious in Clewiston, Florida. An antiquated ordinance bars candidates and their staff from playing chess to pass time.

Scrabble-loving citizens beware of Atwoodville, Connecticut. A local ordinance bans voters from playing Scrabble while waiting for a politician to start a speech.

Statesboro, Georgia, is tough on the more creative women voters. City fathers took it upon themselves even to cover knitting with a special ordinance. A woman isn't permitted to do any knitting while listening to a politician give a speech.

And the small community of Burdickville, Rhode Island, has an unusual ordinance regarding political speeches. City fathers have outlawed citizens from dozing off during a campaign speech given in the daytime. Nothing is mentioned in the law about falling asleep while listening to a boring politician speak at night!

Then there are those odd laws covering food and candidates. Candidates running for public office in

Preston, Idaho, must be careful when it comes to consuming raw onions. They can't do this just before speaking before a large group of voters within the city limits.

And it's also against the law in Kennewick, Washington, for any politician to be seen eating a chocolate ice cream cone while going door-to-door in an effort to greet voters.

Unusual laws also exist which affect voters and food. Anyone who gets an urge to eat some popcorn can forget it if they happen to be a voter in Crookston, Minnesota. A special ordinance bans voters from nibbling on popcorn while listening to a politician speak.

No person is allowed to carry "a sack of Spanish peanuts" to a political rally in Sidney, Ohio. Nor can anyone chew such peanuts while a candidate is talking.

And it's also illegal in Grayling, Michigan, for citizens to eat watermelon at a political rally while waiting for a politician to make a speech.

According to a little-known ordinance in Morgantown, West Virginia, candidates for public office are prohibited from dipping snuff while paying a visit to the local school and talking to the children.

And in Roswell, New Mexico, no political candidate can be caught taking a plug of chewing tobacco just before making a campaign speech.

Jonesboro, Louisiana, has an unusual bit of loony legislation that could be the ruination of many political candidates. Politicians are prohibited from giving speeches lasting longer than ten minutes on weekdays and five minutes on a Sunday.

And this wonderful old piece of legalese should just about eliminate campaign speeches from the political scene. Can you believe that politicians are banned from "telling tall tales and fabricated stories" while giving a campaign speech in Waterbury, Vermont?

San Angelo, Texas, lawmakers passed a loony law of concern to all political candidates or those already in office. Every campaigner must wear long pants when walking down any city street and shaking hands with prospective voters. Anyone found doing this while attired in shorts will be fined and possibly jailed.

Don't ever try to hold a wrestling match as a means of raising much-needed funds for a political candidate in Middleboro, Massachusetts. It's illegal to raise funds in this manner for any person who is running for public office.

There seems to have been a problem with political hucksters in Plunkettville, Oklahoma, some years ago. People in the community evidently became tired of being disturbed by politicians knocking on their doors in the middle of the night. A special ordinance was passed that allowed politicians still to knock on doors—but the knocking could be done only between 8:00 A.M. and 8:00 P.M.

A loony law in Vernal, Utah, is of grave concern to all people who are campaigning for public office. All political candidates are prohibited from knocking on doors and disturbing local citizens prior to 6:00 A.M.

And in Midway, Delaware, a politician must carefully check his or her watch before starting a day of campaigning. Would you believe that political candidates in this quiet little community can't legally start backslapping, handshaking, and talking to potential voters before 8:00 A.M?

An odd clothing law can still be found in Hot Springs, South Dakota. This ordinance bans a female from being seen standing or sitting near a candidate at a political rally unless she's wearing "a long dress that covers her ankles while she is seated in a chair."

Even what a politician can read is covered by a loony law. No candidate for public office in Winfield, Alabama, is allowed to read comic books while sitting in front of a gas station while church services are in session.

Clothing may play an important part in a politician's success—at least in winning a campaign. It's against the law in Fairfield, Illinois, for a candidate for public office to wear a shirt without buttons running up the front.

Some Nebraska people may find they have a difficult time getting to the polls and casting their vote. McCook voters, for example, are prohibited from wearing roller skates when going to the voting precinct on election day.

Politicians in Tennessee are prohibited from involving themselves in a duel with another political candidate or a voter who disagrees with them. And anyone who enters into a duel is banned from holding any elected or appointed office in the Volunteer State.

119

"No child under the age of thirteen years shall be found pitching horseshoes on Decoration Day, or any other holiday, and by so doing, ignore any orator who is presently holding public office, or is a candidate for public office. Such frivolity is deemed unlawful when undertaken within hearing distance of said orator." (New Hampshire statute)

12

Odd and Unusual Laws
Throughout American History

Horse stealing was always a most serious offense in the American Southwest. Stringing the thief up to the nearest tree was the usual penalty. But horse thievery was actually legal in the Oklahoma Territory under certain circumstances. A man was allowed to steal another man's horse when he was being "pursued by a band of renegade Indians."

The first automobile drivers were notorious for hitting pedestrians and for scaring horses. Tennessee legislators became so alarmed in the early 1900s that they passed a special law dealing with the problem. Any man who planned to drive his automobile on a road or a highway within the state was required to warn the public one week in advance! How? By taking out an advertisement in the local newspaper.

An old Chicago, Illinois, law spelled out exactly what kind of eyewear the driver of an automobile had to have while out on the road. Since 1902, all Chicago drivers have been required to wear "spectacles or goggles." Specifically banned were "pince-nez glasses."

During the Civil War, profanity was forbidden for officers serving in the Union army. Union officers were fined one dollar for each swearword they uttered within earshot of the enlisted men.

An old law in Oregon, dating from the frontier gold-rush days, prohibited people of Chinese ancestry from owning land anywhere in the state. Nor was any "Chinaman" allowed to work his own mining claim.

Lawmakers in 1907 Glencoe, Illinois, were fearful of potential automobile speeds in the community. They passed an ordinance requiring every street and road in the community to have "humps." These humps prevented the horseless carriages of that day from going too fast!

New York City passed a law in 1832 requiring all trains to switch over from a steam engine to horses upon reaching the boundaries of Harlem. The horses would then proceed to pull the train to each of its regular stops in New York City. Why the switchover? At that time steam-driven engines were erroneously considered to be much too dangerous to allow in heavily populated areas of the city.

Also in the 1830s, Washington, D.C., passed its "Red Flag" ordinance. The prevailing popular sentiment at the time was that the steam boilers on automobiles were in danger of blowing up at any given moment. The law required a three-man crew for each steam-driven vehicle. One of these men had to walk sixty yards in front of the steam-powered automobile while he waved a red warning flag. The law also set a maximum speed of five miles per hour in open, sparsely traveled areas, and two miles per hour in the more congested parts of the nation's capital.

Years ago, Berkeley, California, had a monumental rat infestation problem in the city sewer system. A special ordinance was passed. Periodically, all bath-tubs in the city—both household and in hotels—were all filled and then emptied at the same time. This would, hopefully, drown all the rats that made their home in the sewer.

Every airplane flying into or out of Jacksonville, Florida, had to be equipped with a "harmonious horn" and a "reliable brake." This 1908 ordinance also required a parachute—not for the pilot or any of the passengers, but for the airplane itself!

123

Right after the Revolutionary War, a federal statute was passed relating to camp followers who covered their business dealings by purporting to be washing the clothing of the military forces. The wording of the legislation was courteous so as not to be offensive to anyone: "Women shall not be allowed to accompany troops as laundresses."

The Volunteer State had a law requiring that each county in Tennessee have its own ranger. The ranger's job had been mandated by the state constitution ever since 1870. At that time, there was a lot of open range throughout Tennessee. Appointed by the county court, the ranger had these duties: round up all stray livestock, board them, find the owner, and charge him with the board bill. The pay of a county ranger? Zero!

All trains running in Colorado, Wyoming, Arizona, Nevada, and other Western states were once required to put out all their lights when passing through a town at night. Why? Because drunken cowboys were notorious for making a game of shooting out the lights on a passing train.

An old law found in Prentiss County, Mississippi, gave a husband the legal right to beat his wife: "The disciplining of a married woman by her husband is in

124

accord with his fundamental right to chastise her. When wives are permitted to disobey their husbands with impunity, the stability of the marriage is threatened."

The above legislation sounds as bad as the old Alabama law specifying a man could beat his spouse with a stick "no bigger around than his thumb." Or the old ordinance in Los Angeles whereby a husband was allowed to whip his loving mate with a leather belt provided the belt was no wider than two inches. Or the law in Arkansas whereby a man was allowed to beat his wife once each month.

Women in colonial Massachusetts were required to make all of their own clothing. All dresses had to be long enough to completely cover the buckles on her shoes. On top of all this, "no garment is to be made whereby the nakedness of the arm may be discovered."

A special law covering the New England colonies was passed regarding estates and wearing apparel. If a person's estate wasn't valued at more than 200 pounds, that individual was severely restricted as to what he or she could wear in public. Such a man or woman was prohibited from wearing lace that cost

125

more than "two shillings a year." Nor could the person wear "gold or silver buttons."

Colonial Virginia was no paradise for people who didn't go to church regularly. The law was severe and actually allowed the death penalty under certain circumstances. This dire punishment was reserved for anyone who missed going to church on three consecutive Sundays. But fortunately, such extreme retribution was seldom carried out.

The New England Colonies were really rough on thieves. Getting caught stealing a first time might bring the culprit to the stocks, many strokes of the lash, or possibly both. But getting caught stealing a second time brought the wrath of the judicial system down on the culprit's head. The value of the object stolen had no bearing on the penalty. Second offenders were simply marched straight to the gallows. There, to the catcalls of the spectators, a noose was slipped over the thief's head and he was hanged until dead.

The lone exception to the above law in Colonial New England was a thief who stole cabbage from a neighbor's field. A cabbage stealer had to stand in the pillory with a fresh head of cabbage sitting atop his head. He'd stay there until the cabbage rotted and fell to the ground.

The most prevalent form of punishment in many of the Colonies was the lash. Sentences differed according to the guilty person's status. For example, acting or speaking disrespectfully in public was punished in Pennsylvania with a sentence of forty lashes for a common laborer. But if the lawbreaker was considered to be a gentleman, he'd simply be placed in the stocks.

Colonial Maryland was tough on citizens who used profanity. Cursing God was sometimes punished by boring a hole in the tongue of the lawbreaker with a red-hot poker. For a second offense, a branding iron was used to sear a letter *B* in the guilty party's forehead. Should the person be stupid enough to be overheard cursing God a third time, he or she was automatically given the death penalty.

The law was strict in colonial New York under the administration of the Earl of Bellomont. Any "Popish priest" who dared to come to New York voluntarily was immediately hanged. So much for early religious freedoms!

The Massachusetts Bay Colony was an awful place to live for some individuals. A person could actually be sentenced to death for nothing more than an accusation of "worshipping any other God but the true God."

The sale of "cakes and sweet buns" was forbidden except for special occasions in colonial Massachusetts and other New England colonies. Why such a silly law? Because the men who wrote and passed the law deemed this would prevent women from getting together and gossiping over tea and cakes.

Every colony had laws against wives who nagged their husbands in public. How was the nagging legally stopped? Simple! Any woman who had the audacity to do this to her husband was given some time in the stocks.

Colonial Virginia had an unusual tax to cover the cost of recording marriages, births, and burials with the vestry clerk. All it took was five pounds of tobacco.

Men who were observed kissing their wives in public on the Sabbath were punished in the Massachusetts Bay Colony. The law was especially enforced in the city of Boston, where the affectionate fellow was penalized with two hours in the stocks for a first

128

offense. Fair or not, the woman wasn't punished for her husband's misdeed.

Seventeenth-century Connecticut required the death penalty for a variety of infractions of the law. For example, the death penalty could actually be imposed for "disobeying a parent," or for being "a stubborn and rebellious son."

Colonial Maryland wasn't at all lenient when it came to tobacco stealing. The penalty for this kind of theft, regardless of the amount, was death by hanging.

There was even a law that banned the celebration of Christmas for a period of twenty-two years. It all began on May 11, 1659, in the Massachusetts Bay Colony. Members of the colonial legislature were relentless in their uncompromising stand against Christmas, which was considered to be no more than a pagan holiday. Dominated by Puritans, this law-making body passed a harsh anti-Christmas law. The unique legislation was worded thus: "Whosoever shall be found observing any such day as Christmas . . . shall pay for every offense five shillings." A citizen was also in big trouble on Christmas if he "read common prayer, danced, played cards or played any musical instrument except the drum, trumpet, or Jew's harp."

"The Director General and Council of New Netherlands in order to prevent accidents do hereby ordain that no Wagons, Carts or Sleighs shall be run, rode or driven at a gallop within this city." (New York City law, June 27, 1652)

III

COURTROOM CAPERS

13

Ridiculous Rulings and Courtroom Cases

A sorry-looking Aberdeen, South Dakota, man stood before the magistrate, who was giving him a verbal shellacking. The judge boomed: "What's the matter with you? Can't you behave yourself for one week? You've been before this court at least thirty times. You've been charged with drunkenness, panhandling, shoplifting, assault, and now—now you're accused of beating your wife! What do you have to say for yourself?"

The hapless fellow shifted uneasily and shrugged, saying: "Gee, Your Honor, nobody's perfect."

In Dyersburg, Tennessee, a bigamist, married to eight different women, told the judge he didn't smoke, drink, or use profanity. "My only vice," he explained, "is that whenever I see a pretty woman I can't resist asking her to marry me and be my wife."

The judge gave him three years in which to build up his resistance.

A woman was arrested in Dexter, Maine, for stealing a shopping cart from a supermarket. In court, she won an acquittal by pointing out that a sign over the multitude of carts said: PLEASE TAKE ONE.

A Norfolk, Nebraska, judge fined a woman $2.50 for crossing the street against a red light. She paid the clerk with a $5 bill but didn't wait for change. The judge noticed this and remarked that she should wait for her money. "That's okay," she said, "I got to cross back to the other side."

A Williamsport, Pennsylvania, man who annoyed his wife was ordered to travel 1,200 miles in any direction, sending postcards back to the judge every 200 miles to demonstrate his obedience.

An astute lawyer in Seaford, Delaware, received a distress call some years ago from a luckless client whom police had arrested for arson. With plenty of damaging evidence in the hands of the authorities, things looked dark. Yet the attorney evinced such confidence during the preliminary proceedings that the prosecutor began to have doubts. It came as a distinct relief to him when the lawyer offered: "If you'll drop the arson charge, my client will plead guilty to attempted arson."

The prosecutor consented and the judge approved the agreement. But when it came time to impose the sentence, the lawyer blandly called the judge's attention to a peculiar problem of arithmetic. According to a newly passed state law, the penalty for any attempted crime should be half the penalty for a completed crime. And the penalty for arson was life imprisonment.

"How long," inquired the lawyer, "is half of a man's life? The Scripture tells us that we knoweth not the day nor the hour of our departure. Will this court sentence the prisoner to half of a minute—or to half of the days of Methuselah?"

Stumped for a few moments, the judge finally decided to set the defendant free.

In Richmond, a broad-minded judge let petty offenders roll a huge pair of dice to determine the number of days they would get in jail. After the judge's death, his secret came out: the dice were loaded.

A jury in Craig, Colorado, inquiring into a case of suicide, listened to the evidence and brought in this verdict: "The jury is of one mind—temporarily insane."

A man in Hamilton, Ohio, was summoned to the witness stand to tell all he knew about a shooting fracas.

"Did you see the shot fired?" asked the judge.

"No," was the reply, "but I heard it."

"Evidence unsatisfactory," snapped the judge. "Step down."

The man obediently headed toward his seat. But as he mused about legal technicalities, he couldn't restrain a derisive snicker.

Outraged, the judge ordered him back to the stand.

"How dare you laugh like that in my courtroom?" thundered the judge.

"Your Honor," the witness asked calmly, "did you see me laugh?"

"No," sputtered the judge, "but I distinctly heard you."

"Evidence unsatisfactory."

The judge relented.

Who's winning the battle of the sexes? Draw your own conclusions. A beautiful plaintiff, suing in a Grand Rapids, Michigan, courtroom, won the judge's permission to display her knees to the all-male jury even though they became "unduly excited in her behalf."

A couple from Anniston, Alabama, were on their way to get married. They got lost and called the Justice of the Peace for directions from a service station to the courthouse. He told them to stay where they were, then drove over and married them alongside the gas pumps.

A man in Boise, Idaho, was hauled into court for beating his wife. The judge stepped down from the bench and promptly floored the defendant with a looping right hook to the jaw.

The defendant in an Atlantic City case seemed trapped in a mesh of circumstantial evidence until his lawyer addressed the jury: "Once upon a time, a farmer's son sneaked into the kitchen for a bite to eat. Finding a freshly baked pie, he ate it all. Just then Tom, the house cat, came along. The boy rubbed the cat's paws in the remains of the pie, letting it make tracks out of the kitchen. Then he returned to his chores in the cornfield.

"Soon," the lawyer continued, "he saw his father go to the woods with a covered box and a shotgun. There was the report of the gun. The farmer reappeared, his box empty. The boy leaned on his hoe and said, 'Poor Tom! You were a victim of circumstantial evidence!' "

The defendant was acquitted.

A housewife in Thermopolis, Wyoming, was arrested for assault with a deadly weapon. She won an acquittal and the court's hearty congratulations for swatting an aggressive bill collector with a baseball bat.

Taking due note of a thief's plea that he had acted under hypnosis, a Worcester, Massachusetts, judge told him to get hypnotized again—so he wouldn't mind spending ten years in jail.

Three gypsies in Orlando, Florida, were arrested on a charge of "obscene dancing," to wit: "a lewd and lascivious contortion of the stomach." They cleared themselves in court with the argument that "the stomach is a small abdominal sac whose contortions are visible only from inside the body."

In Kankakee, Illinois, a young woman had a masher arrested for calling her a chicken. The judge ascertained the plaintiff's weight and calculated exactly what she would cost if she really were a chicken. He fixed that sum as the man's fine.

A rural judge near Spartansburg, South Carolina, at the close of arguments, said importantly to the opposing attorneys: "I will take this case under advisement until next Monday, at which time I will render judgment for the plaintiff."

A lawyer instructed his pretty young client, on trial for shoplifting in Albany, New York, to burst into tears every time he thumped the table. This she did. However, while the attorney was arguing a point, he tapped the table by mistake. His client obediently started to sob. Puzzled, the judge exclaimed: "What's the matter?"

Tearfully, the young woman blurted out the truth: "My lawyer told me to cry every time he knocked on the table."

Derisive laughter swept the courtroom. But the lawyer turned adversity into opportunity. To the jury, he

139

said: "Gentlemen, how can you reconcile the idea of crime with such childish candor and simplicity?"

The jury found her not guilty.

A St. Louis man was accused of selling whiskey to the Indians. He claimed he didn't know the law because he couldn't read. The judge sentenced him to jail until he could pass a reading test. The judge also sent a thief to the same cell to serve as the teacher. The pair buckled down to work, and the illiterate fellow graduated in three weeks.

A singer and a bandleader went to court in Lafayette, Louisiana, to settle a contract dispute. The legal issues were complex, and the judge, after announcing his decision, suddenly burst into song, crooning a few bars of "April Showers." He explained to the startled litigants: "I just wanted you-all to know that I was musically qualified to decide this case."

A jury in Springfield, Missouri, solemnly brought in this verdict: "We, the defendant, find the jury guilty of hog theft."

Some years ago in Yuma, Arizona, a cowboy was tried on a charge of horse stealing. Since the jurors were all Mexicans unfamiliar with English, the proceedings had to be filtered laboriously to them through an interpreter.

Finally, on the afternoon of the third weary day, the cowboy's lawyer arose for his closing argument. But instead of the expected "Gentlemen of the jury," he began: *"Señores jurados."*

The jurors snapped to delighted attention. But the prosecutor leaped to his feet and roared: "I object! English is the official language in this courtroom."

The defense lawyer appealed to the judge in vain. The law was clear: he must speak English. Appearing to be crestfallen, he began his final plea. Equally crestfallen, the jurors resigned themselves to the frustration of secondhand listening. But they had learned something. Now they knew which side insisted on technicalities and which side wanted to talk to them in the way they understood. The verdict came swiftly: "Not guilty!"

As the grateful cowboy left the court, he whispered to his attorney, "I never knew you spoke Spanish."

"I didn't," grinned the lawyer, "until last night. But it was a cinch to learn two little words."

In a Cedar Rapids, Iowa, damage suit, the plaintiff had finished his testimony, during which he'd told several obvious fibs. The judge asked the defendant's attorney if he had any questions he'd like to ask the plaintiff.

"No thank you, Your Honor," the lawyer replied. "I'm quite prepared to let lying dogs sleep."

In Rochester, Minnesota, jurors were being selected to try an accused wife-slayer. One man asked to be excused on the ground that, as a bachelor, he knew very little about women. With a sigh, the judge rejected the plea. His Honor explained that, as a husband, he himself knew even less.

A farmer in Barre, Vermont, was hauled into court after dumping a load of garbage in front of the town hall. But the case was dismissed when he said he was simply getting even with townspeople who threw beer bottles and tin cans into his fields.

In Athens, Georgia, a convicted felon succeeded in getting the judge to cut his jail sentence from thirteen years to twelve years, by reminding His Honor that thirteen is an unlucky number.

An assistant district attorney in Oklahoma City was questioning an obstinate witness who, in replying, insisted on addressing all his answers directly back to the attorney.

"Witness, speak to the jury!" the judge ordered testily.

The man turned, looked the jury over, nodded affably, and said, "Howdy."

A rock musician in South Bend, Indiana, was charged with cruelty to animals after coating his cat with luminous paint. He was acquitted when he testified he did it to avoid stepping on the cat's tail in the dark.

A charge of forgery against an elderly man was dismissed in a Santa Fe, New Mexico, court after witnesses testified the defendant couldn't write!

A prosecutor in Beaumont, Texas, became disgusted with the tactics of an opposing lawyer. "Don't you think," he asked the judge point-blank, "that defense counsel is the greatest liar you ever saw?"

"I wouldn't say that," parried the judge, "but he certainly wrestles with the truth harder than any other lawyer on the circuit."

In a Juneau, Alaska, courtroom, a witness had the irritating habit of answering questions almost before

143

they were asked. Finally, the judge asked a question of his own:

"Are you the same Mr. . . ."

"Yes!" broke in the witness.

"—who was hanged yesterday?"

A man was arrested for possession of a dangerous weapon in Bowling Green, Kentucky. He was acquitted after testifying that the blackjack he owned was a sentimental gift from his mother.

A dog thief in Cumberland, Maryland, calmly reminded the judge of the common law rule that dogs have no legal value. The judge went ahead and found the defendant guilty of stealing the dog's collar.

A woman in Jonesboro, Arkansas, was arrested for selling onions on Sunday. The local blue laws forbade the sale of vegetables on Sunday. However, the sale of "fruit" was allowed. The judge concluded that the woman was innocent because "an onion can sometimes take the place of a fruit, especially at dessert!"

A housewife in Hattiesburg, Mississippi, was arrested for being a garrulous nuisance. She was ordered to observe two-and-a-half hours of strict silence.

144

Six jurors in a Spokane, Washington, case turned in these ballots: No. 1—"Assault and Battery"; No. 2—"Salt and Battery"; Nos. 3 and 4—"Gilty of Salt Only"; No. 5—"No cose of Action"; No. 6—"No Action of Cose."

The reason that he stole the water meter and then reported the theft to the police, the man told the court in Wilmington, North Carolina, was because he had eight kids and wanted to go to jail to "get some peace and quiet."

"Four months," the judge said—then suspended the sentence "in view of this man's responsibility toward his large family."

> "Property must not be taken without compensation, but . . . some property may be taken or destroyed for public use without paying for it, if you do not take too much." (*Springer* case; Oliver Wendell Holmes, 1928 ruling)

14

Ludicrous Lawsuits

In Manchester, New Hampshire, a jittery landlord filed suit to evict a tenant on the ground that the tenant's brother, long since dead, was haunting the house. The court refused to evict, explaining that as long as the tenant kept on paying the rent, his brother's ghost had the legal right to hang around.

When a Fort Smith, Arkansas, gambler died at a roulette table in Las Vegas, the game kept on without interruption. No one noticed that the dead man's bet still stood on Number 17. Later, his widow sued the casino for the half-million dollars won by the lucky stiff.

An Oklahoman who was fond of ghosts bought a gloomy old mansion in Tulsa on the assurance that it was haunted by an Elizabethan lady. When the lady's ghost failed to make an appearance, he complained to the local court. The court ruled he was entitled to damages because he hadn't gotten his money's worth.

In Eau Claire, Wisconsin, a medical group sued a man who had promised them his body for research. They charged that he had broken his promise by having two of his teeth pulled without their permission.

In Norwich, Connecticut, a shop owner claimed compensation for a loss of business incurred when the weatherman wrongly predicted rain, thus scaring tourists away from a local festival.

A Grand Junction, Colorado, baker sued a woman for slander. The lady claimed she could tell he kneaded his bread with his feet because it had his footprints on it.

In Alexandria, Louisiana, a housewife sued for auto injuries. She charged that the accident made her forget how to cook her husband's favorite dish—steak and kidney pie.

A female passenger from Jamesville, Ohio, sued a steamship line for giving her toy poodle an inferiority complex! How? They had placed him in a cage between a growling police dog and a barking Great Dane.

147

A man from Pearl City, Hawaii, claimed compensation for an injury he got while drinking in a tavern. It seems his foot skidded off the bar's brass rail.

In Dodge City, Kansas, a dead man's heirs sued to prevent burial of the body until they collected the inheritances provided in a will tattooed on his chest.

In Clarksdale, Mississippi, a man hastily sold his business at a loss. The fellow then sued his doctor when he failed to die as the physician had predicted.

In Phillipsburg, New Jersey, a man had to pay his stenographer $2,200 for telling her such a funny story that she swallowed some paper clips she was holding in her mouth.

In Des Moines, a professional gambler was injured in an auto accident. He claimed damages for "injury to my ability to make four the hard way with dice."

A woman in Millinocket, Maine, sued a painter for damages. She complained that when she criticized his work, the fellow painted her arms yellow.

In Lexington, Kentucky, a poet sued his landlord, complaining that the landlord's mule had sneaked into his room. Seems the animal had thoughtlessly gobbled up a stack of unpublished manuscripts.

A businessman in Bakersfield, California, had a Siamese twin detained in a legal dispute. The other twin sued him for false arrest.

Two men in Jamestown, North Dakota, sued a railroad for $10,000. It seems their train had arrived at the racetrack too late for them to clean up on the daily double.

A missing sailor from Annapolis, Maryland, was declared dead by a court. He later turned up alive to find that all of his property had been divided among relatives. Despite a ten-year siege of the courts, he never came back to legal life—except in one place. His existence was cheerfully acknowledged by the Internal Revenue Service!

A woman in Rockhill, South Carolina, sued a man for insulting her. So persuasively did she ask for $4,000 in damages that the jury gave her $4,500.

In Midland, Michigan, a disenchanted former college student sued his alma mater for failing to teach him wisdom.

149

In Selma, Alabama, a watchman with a hearing disability sought back pay. He simply wanted the money due him for the ten days he kept working after he had failed to hear his boss say, "You're fired!"

In Great Falls, Montana, a woman sued a neighbor for using abusive language. She claimed $75 damages—minus a $45 credit for the abusive language she used in return.

In a Scranton, Pennsylvania, restaurant a woman bit into an oyster and found a pearl worth $750. Both she and the restaurant owner hustled into court to claim ownership of the pearl. The judge ruled with strict impartiality. He awarded the pearl to the gentleman who had paid for the woman's dinner.

In Flagstaff, Arizona, a man sued the corner grocer for alienating his dog's affections! How? Simply by encouraging a romance with the grocer's dog.

In Middletown, Rhode Island, a theatergoer sued a hypnotist. He claimed that a volunteer from the audience was hypnotized into thinking he was a monkey. The fellow swung down from the stage and took a bite out of the claimant's hat.

In Watertown, New York, a woman sued her landlord. She claimed the man caused her to fall down from shock when he called her "sweetheart" on the telephone.

A man in Ely, Nevada, sued an auto dealer for $30,000. Why? Because he claimed that the suspense of waiting for delivery of his new car had given him ulcers.

A man in Macon, Georgia, failed to get an answer to his letter of inquiry. He sued for the postage stamp he had enclosed for the reply.

In Kokomo, Indiana, a man retrieved a valuable pearl swallowed by a dog. He claimed compensation for the reduction in the pearl's size due to acids in the dog's stomach.

How responsible is the brewer for the behavior of corks in his bottled products? A federal judge in Portland, Oregon, was asked to decide. He ruled: "Beer is expected to contain gas sufficient to exert considerable pressure. Gas, therefore, is legitimately present. And with the cap removed, it is inevitable the cork will pop. So since the presence of gas was known, the cap, until removed, had held the cork in place. The cork had acted as expected. Obviously nothing had gone wrong. There was no sign of negligence. Therefore, the popping cork that hit John A.

151

Winkler of Klamath Falls in the eye was not the fault of the Star Brewing Company. Mr. Winkler may not sue."

An embittered man sued God for $800 in back tithes. Apparently God did not deliver on a Miami, Florida, pastor's promise that "blessings and awards would come to the person" who gave 10 percent of his wealth to his church. When neither blessing nor award surfaced after a three-year waiting period, the forty-nine-year old plumber decided to "invest" his money elsewhere. He went to court to get back his money.

A court in Caldwell, Idaho, declined to award damages to a woman who had to go to a psychiatrist for treatment. She claimed that her washing machine, in its spin cycle, had pursued her around her utility room.

A widow in Clarksburg, West Virginia, sued a railroad for damages. She charged that sparks from the train had set her house on fire. At the trial, the railroad's attorney scoffed at her claim: "Our records show that the train was in the station four minutes. As it was leaving, the crew saw this house *already burning*. It must have been on fire *before* the train arrived. A fire couldn't grow big enough to see in only four minutes."

The widow's lawyer arose and laid a large gold watch on the knee of the jury foreman. He said, "Please keep track and tell us when four minutes have passed."

A hush settled over the courtroom as the moments dragged by interminably. The tension became almost unbearable until the foreman announced that the four minutes were over. Convinced, the jury turned down the railroad's claim and awarded the widow a substantial settlement.

A farmer in North Platte, Nebraska, became embroiled in a nasty lawsuit with a neighbor. He informed his lawyer that he planned to send a brace of fine ducks to the judge. The lawyer was horrified. He warned the farmer: "Don't or you'll lose the case for sure."

After the farmer won his case, he told his startled lawyer that he had sent the ducks after all. He added with a chuckle: "But I signed my neighbor's name."

In Kansas City, Missouri, a man slipped at the entrance to his place of employment and later died of his injuries. His widow's claim for compensation was turned down because, although his arm had been reaching for the company doorknob, his right foot—

the one that did the slipping—had been on a public sidewalk.

"Because of extreme fear of being shot to death, I was forced to swim several irrigation canals, attempt to swim a 'raging' Jordan River, and expose myself to innumerable bites by many insects. At one point, I heard a volley of shotgun blasts, and this completed my anxiety." So claimed Walter Wood, convicted murderer and escapee from the Utah State Prison. He sued the state for $2,000,000 when apprehended.

15

Grounds for Divorce: A Woman's Perspective

Divorce is never really funny. But some of the flim-flam excuses for breaking the matrimonial knot are! Many people certainly don't pay much attention to the scriptural admonitions of Paul, who said: ". . . Let not the wife depart from her husband . . . and let not the husband put away his wife." The course of true love doesn't always run smoothly. And sometimes it can be darned strange, as these cases show.

A woman in Caribou, Maine, sued her husband for divorce because he did all the housework. She charged in court that she didn't clean house, grocery shop, or slave over a hot stove cooking at any time during their thirteen years of marriage. Hubby refused to allow her to do any of these things! She further claimed she hated living on a pedestal. The woman was charging her husband with cruelty. She lost! The divorce court judge ruled the husband "had been tactless, not cruel."

A woman in Marshfield, Wisconsin, had a husband who once promised to pay her $1 per kiss while they were married. Her divorce suit asked the court to award her $3,000 in back payments!

You think you've got troubles? Because her husband shot tin cans off her head with a slingshot, and sometimes with a pistol, a Frackville, Pennsylvania, wife asked to be given her much-desired freedom.

A woman in Crawfordsville, Indiana, requested a divorce on her complaint that her husband made a habit of bringing his pals into their bathroom. He always did it while she was relaxing in the bathtub!

In Bellows Falls, Vermont, a woman told the judge she wanted a divorce because of a parrot. Seems her spouse taught his pet parrot to shout at her every morning. And what did the parrot yell? "Get up, darn you, get up!"

In Strawberry Plains, Tennessee, a woman charged in her divorce suit that she often served steak and onions for dinner. The problem? Her husband had his own ideas about sharing. He ate all the steak and left her with the onions!

156

A woman in Bullhead, South Dakota, filed for a divorce because her husband hit her with a chicken when she refused to cook it!

In filing for a divorce, a Margaretsville, North Carolina, wife charged her husband had a "vile and ungovernable temper." She said he would upset the checkerboard whenever he saw he might lose the game.

A woman in Canon City, Colorado, petitioned for a divorce on the grounds that her husband forced her to duck under the dashboard whenever he drove past a girlfriend.

A woman in Flanders, New Jersey, asked for a divorce decree on the testimony that her husband repeatedly stood her on her head! And he once brought home an inebriated sailor and put him in their bathtub to sleep it off.

An Ellensburg, Washington, woman sued for divorce. The charge? Hubby put fishhooks in his pants pockets each night when he went to bed.

A woman in Susanville, California, sued her husband for divorce and charged him with selling the kitchen stove in order to get money with which he purchased drinks. The man readily admitted the charge. But he begged the court for leniency on the ground his wife was such a terrible housekeeper she didn't even miss the stove for two weeks!

The charge against the Effingham, Illinois, man appearing in divorce court was desertion. With rather impressive earnestness, the defendant faced the judge and said: "Judge, if you knew my wife like I know her, you wouldn't call me a deserter. I'm not a deserter! I'm a refugee!" His wife had no trouble getting her divorce.

Even false teeth can be the cause for a divorce in some homes. A woman in Enid, Oklahoma, charged in divorce court that her husband was so stingy he insisted on her wearing his old false teeth!

A woman in Hutchinson, Kansas, filed for divorce on the grounds that her husband made her do all her reading in a closet. Why? So his slumber wouldn't be disturbed!

A woman in Casa Grande, Arizona, filed to divorce her husband, whose custom it was to leave her at a cheap movie while he went on to the more expensive one.

A blushing bride hauled her husband into a Batavia, New York, divorce court for insisting on too many kisses. The judge got a signed pledge from the amorous husband. The fellow agreed to limit his kisses to five before lunch and five more before dinner.

In Winnemucca, Nevada, a woman saw a letter in her husband's handwriting in the postman's hand. She snatched it away and tore it open. She found it was a love letter to another woman. The wife sued for divorce and won. But she was fined $20 for tampering with the mail!

A woman in Galena, Alaska, told the court that the man she married insisted they sleep in a hammock. In twenty-three years of married life, she complained, she'd fallen out of the hammock sixteen times. She felt she was getting much too old for such insecure sleeping arrangements.

A Loving, New Mexico, woman filed for a divorce because her husband made her address him by his military title of major and salute him whenever he passed.

A fifty-three-year-old woman in Mountain Home, Idaho, filed a divorce petition against her seventy-three-year-old husband. In it she charged the man "sleeps in his underwear and seldom changes. He spits in the sink and cuts his toenails in the living room.

He has amassed his fortune by doing such penny-pinching things as wearing secondhand clothes, turning off the gas and lights, and not giving the dog and cat enough to eat." The judge dismissed the petition saying the husband's behavior was insufficient grounds. Why? Because "he had *always* been mean, frugal, careful, or whatever you call it."

A distraught woman in Flasher, North Dakota, didn't consider her husband's attentions when she was ill as being properly solicitous. She sought a divorce, charging that during her illness her husband sent an undertaker to see her, and he also ordered funeral wreaths.

It wasn't the "other woman" who broke up a marriage in Hardwick, Georgia. A matron, suing for divorce, complained that her spouse "stayed home too much and was much too affectionate."

A professional fighter's wife in Huntsville, Alabama, begged the court for a divorce. She claimed she was tired of being used as his sparring partner.

In Starkville, Mississippi, a woman filed a divorce action because, she charged, her husband sprinkled snuff on her and then hit her with a head of raw cabbage.

A woman in Lynch Heights, Delaware, wanted her freedom based on her unusual courtroom testimony. She charged her husband with cruelty—he continually put itching powder in her bras and panties when she wasn't looking.

In Amherst, Massachusetts, a woman complained in divorce court that her husband demanded money from her. He wanted $3.50 an hour for doing odd jobs around the house!

A woman in Narrows, Virginia, filed for divorce and demanded financial compensation for the loss of her virginity. The woman's loss of virginity was held by the court to be a natural consequence of marriage. It didn't require any kind of reparations from the former husband.

A woman in Cut Bank, Montana, wanted her freedom because her husband apparently didn't trust her. Upon leaving for his office each day, the fellow marked the soles of her shoes with white chalk so he could tell whether or not she strayed from home.

In Cranston, Rhode Island, a woman sought a divorce by complaining that her husband was a murder-story buff. Seems most of her evenings were taken up by lying on the floor as the "corpse" while he tried to reconstruct the crime.

A woman in Thibodaux, Louisiana, married a certain Jean Joseph. She later found his real name to be Jean Louise—a notorious confidence man. He had borrowed the Jean Joseph identity from a man who had died four years earlier. But when she sued for divorce, the court turned her down on the ground that there is no legal way to divorce a dead man.

In Denton, Texas, an estranged wife demanded temporary alimony for a blood transfusion. Her husband, short of money, offered to donate his blood instead. The wife indignantly refused to accept "that man's blood." After due deliberation, the judge arranged for the husband to make a blood deposit—and the wife to make a blood withdrawal—at the local blood bank.

Santa Claus the reason for a divorce? Yes! A woman in Pendleton, Oregon, filed for a divorce because her husband never gave her any Christmas presents! Why? "Because," she claimed, "he remains serenely confident that Santa Claus would bring them."

16

Grounds for Divorce: A Man's Perspective

District Judge Keith Hayes of Las Vegas, Nevada, once granted divorces to fifteen couples in fifteen minutes. Explained Hayes: "I just don't have the time to spend all morning on divorce cases, so I decided to get them all out of the way at one time." Judge Hayes may have a valid point, as you can readily see after you peruse the following daffy divorce actions from all around the United States:

A man in Tarittville, Connecticut, came into court seeking a divorce. When the judge asked him what his grounds were, the disgruntled husband simply handed him a note he'd received from his wife: "I won't be home when you return from work. Have gone to the bridge club. There'll be a recipe for your dinner at 7 o'clock on Channel 2."

A new bride in Rock Springs, Wyoming, right after the marital knot was safely tied, admitted she had trapped her husband into matrimony strictly for his money. In the subsequent divorce action brought about by the angry husband, the court ruled he had no kick coming. The judge explained: "The game laws of this state provide no closed season against this kind of trapping. Divorce denied!"

An elderly man in Batesville, Arkansas, sued his fifteen-year-old wife for divorce. His complaint? He was upset because "she always acted like a child"!

A divorce was requested by a husband in Wood River Junction, Rhode Island. He testified that his wife had deliberately used prize specimens from his butterfly collection to trim her spring bonnet.

Doubting the sincerity of his wife's vows, a Point Charlotte, Florida, man filed for divorce immediately after the wedding. He said that he and his wife had hardly departed the altar when she took him to her favorite bar. There she collared the bartender, and said, "Well, I told you I'd marry him. Give me the $50."

A man in Price, Utah, asked for a divorce after complaining to the judge that his wife hung photographs of her four ex-husbands in their bedroom over the bed!

164

A supposedly happily married Paw Paw, West Virginia, husband sued his wife for divorce, saying: "I didn't like the way she treated her mother."

A divorce over toothpaste? Seems so, at least in this particular case—a man in Hastings, Nebraska, filed a complaint in divorce court, saying his wife was so lazy he had to squeeze the toothpaste for her.

A divorced husband in Sikeston, Missouri, was awarded $25,000 in damages from the estate of his wife's former lover. Seems that the deceased was liable under Missouri law, even though now dead. The judge said: "The wrongful invasion of a husband's marital rights has no precise market value, and its valuation is a matter about which reasonable persons may and do differ."

A minister in Circleville, Ohio, filed for a divorce from his wife by charging her with cruelty. He specified that every time he began preaching in his church, she would get up and walk out!

And a man in Cambridge, Maryland, believed he was entitled to a divorce. Why? "Because," he declared, "my wife's dumplings always stick to the roof of my mouth."

In Honolulu, a man sued his wife for a divorce over food! He charged that his spouse served pea soup for breakfast and supper. And she even put pea sandwiches in his lunch box to carry to work.

A husband in Hazard, Kentucky, wanted a divorce. Seems his wife would beat him up when he removed the onions from a hamburger without first getting her permission.

The judge hearing a divorce case asked the Montevideo, Minnesota, husband why he thought his wife didn't love him. The husband replied: "Well, Your Honor, I was painting our cellar door and fell down the stairs. My wife rushed to the scene, stared at me sprawled on the cellar floor half-conscious, and said, 'While you're down there, Henry, put some coal in the furnace.'"

In a Battle Creek, Michigan, court a man confessed to pickpocketing. He then promptly filed for divorce. Why? He declared that he had found his wife's picture in the wallet stolen from a sailor!

Testifying against his wife in a divorce suit, a husband in a Laconia, New Hampshire, court said: "When we are at dinner, I have to always be on the alert to make sure I get my fair share."

A deaf man in Bennettsville, South Carolina, was requesting a divorce. The grounds? His wife was always nagging him in sign language!

A man in Cherokee, Iowa, testified in a divorce court that his wife put this sign on their garage: GARAGE FOR RENT AND MAN FOR SALE.

In suing his wife for a divorce, a Pascaqoula, Mississippi, man obtained a temporary injunction restraining her from: striking him; attempting to take his life; hiding the silverware so he couldn't eat; hiding his ash trays; destroying his clothes; forbidding him to watch football games; and barring his friends from their home.

A man in Grants, New Mexico, was denied a divorce, although he proved his wife was guilty of extramarital high jinks. The court reasoned that the husband was partly to blame for the dilemma because, being aware of his wife's yen for other men, he should have "exercised a peculiar vigilance over her."

A wife in Sugarcreek, Pennsylvania, was upheld in her claim of henpecking privileges during her hubby's divorce action. He did not get the requested divorce. The court blamed him for allowing her to get into the tiresome habit!

167

A man in Burns Junction, Oregon, sued his spouse for divorce over her habit of going through his pockets while he slept. The divorce was denied. In fact, the court gave its approval of "her custom of rifling her husband's pockets while he was sleeping off a binge."

A man in Winthrop, Maine, sought a divorce from his wife because she wore earplugs every time his mother came to visit them.

A man in Smelterville, Idaho, sought a divorce on the grounds that his wife tried to scare his mother out of the house. How? She pretended to be a ghost!

A man in Platteville, Wisconsin, was seeking a divorce. He related this incident in court: "My wife took a plane trip and mailed back a $100,000 insurance policy made out to Sandy—the family dog!"

A man in National City, California, became involved in a divorce action when he playfully drew a cartoon on his lover's buttocks and signed his name. His paramour forgot to wash off the drawing; when her husband spotted the autograph, he recognized the signature and filed a complaint. The judge declared that there had never been more clear-cut evidence of guilt in the history of his court.

The judge looked at the man from Anchorage, Alaska, who was seeking to obtain a divorce. "You claim false pretense?" he asked. "Misrepresentation. Isn't that a rather curious reason to want a divorce?" "It's like this, Your Honor," said the harassed husband. "When I asked this woman to marry me, she said she was agreeable. She wasn't!"

A Sulphur, Oklahoma, man requested a divorce because of what his wife did each time they had a quarrel. She would drive past their home in a car equipped with a public-address system that roared, "Mr. Smith, I won't be home tonight! That's final!"

In Sioux Falls, South Dakota, a husband filed for a divorce because his wife had given each of her five stepchildren a saxophone.

A lonely hearts advertisement was the cause of at least one divorce petition. A man in Huntingburg, Indiana, told the court his wife had described herself as five feet four and 118 pounds. They married before actually meeting. When they met, she turned out to be six feet tall and weighed more than 300 pounds.

Sometimes the path of justice in a divorce suit leads right out of this world. A fellow in Topeka, Kansas, filed for a divorce after charging that his wife was

169

carrying on a torrid romance with the ghost of a dead film star.

After twenty-six years of wedded bliss, a man in Winston-Salem, North Carolina, filed for a divorce on the grounds of "irreconcilable differences." What exactly were these differences? The husband was made to run outside the home in his underwear while playing a tambourine whenever his wife wasn't in the mood for lovemaking. However, when she was in the mood, which was once each week, his wife made him pay $8.50 for each sexual encounter.

A fellow in Barton, Vermont, sued his wife for divorce because of "her obsession with jigsaw puzzles." He further explained to the judge: "I am made to spend an average of $440 per month on these puzzles. She spreads them over nearly every square inch of our home."

A young woman in Billings, Montana, was sued for divorce over her artful use of a pair of spectacles to keep her fiancé from finding out she had a glass eye. To his complaint after the wedding, the court replied: "It is not necessary for a woman during courtship to inform her husband-to-be of any device or attachment used to improve the work of nature in the construction of her face or figure."

17

Driving Drivel in the Courtroom

"**B**ut Your Honor," protested the meek little man in Tuscaloosa, Alabama, "I couldn't have passed that red light as the officer charges."

"And why not?" inquired the magistrate.

"My wife was with me, sir, and when she's with me, nothing can appear on the road without her telling me about it—a dog, a cat, and especially a red light. She is unquestionably the finest backseat driver in the world, so you see, Your Honor, it couldn't possibly have happened."

As can be seen in the above example, people will say just about anything when they get caught breaking the law. Some motorists will use almost any excuse or do almost anything in an effort to wiggle off the hook. Here are a few of the funnier excuses offered by those who should have known better.

A schoolteacher in Kirksville, Missouri, was stopped by the police for driving through a red light. She was immediately brought before the judge. Said the magistrate: "So you're a schoolteacher. That's fine. Madam, your presence here fulfills a long-standing desire. For years I've hoped to have a schoolteacher standing there.

"Now," he thundered, "sit down at that table and write 'I went through a red light' 500 times!"

In Sterling, Colorado, a woman was arrested for driving through eight stop signs. What was her excuse? She told the judge she couldn't see the signs! She'd been driving the wrong way on a one-way street!

A motorist in Berlin, New Hampshire, failed to signal for a left turn. He explained to the judge that his turn signal was broken. And, because it was during a local election day, he was afraid to put his hand out lest a candidate would run over and shake it.

A nineteen-year-old man was arrested for auto theft in Tucson, Arizona. The young man explained to the judge how he'd failed his driver's test. So he went about stealing five vehicles—but merely to practice proper driving techniques, as he wished to take the test again.

Said a judge in Marion, Ohio, "You admit seeing this young lady driving toward you. Why didn't you give her half the road?"

"I was going to," the motorist replied, "as soon as I could discover which half she wanted."

A man in Monroe, Louisiana, was stopped for drunken driving. He refused to take a breathalizer test. Why? "Because," he told the judge, "it was not me but my cocker spaniel who was driving."

"I thought there was something terribly wrong," a Scottsbluff, Nebraska, woman told the judge, "because I had to keep on swerving to avoid oncoming cars." She was fined for driving against the traffic on the interstate!

A judge asked a Hardscrabble, Delaware, man why he stole a car when he had one of his own. The fellow tried to explain: "I was drinking, and I was much too intoxicated to drive my own car."

Then there's the man from Pierre, South Dakota, who really deserved a break! He stopped his car on a bridge over the Missouri River. The fellow then dove over the side in order to rescue a woman in the swirling water below. Meanwhile, a police officer came on the scene and wrote him a ticket for illegally parking on a bridge!

An imaginative New Bedford, Massachusetts, woman was arrested for reckless driving. She explained to the judge how she ordinarily drove using celestial navigation. But she claimed to have lost her bearings when she mistook a television tower beacon for the evening star.

Here's how a driving incident was explained to the judge. It all took place in an Ogden, Utah, parking lot: "That young man was in a Porsche when he shot past me," explained the woman, "as I was about to enter a parking spot. He smiled as he announced: 'That's how it's done when you're young and agile.' Well, I didn't like that one little bit, so I rammed his Porsche with my Cadillac and said, 'That's how it's done when you're old and rich.' "

In Rockford, Illinois, a man was arrested for illegally parking in front of a drugstore. He tried to explain to the judge that watching a woman driver had made him so nervous that he had to stop and buy a sedative.

174

A motorist in Beckley, West Virginia, was arrested for almost running down a policeman. At his trial, he acknowledged that he had downed four beers just before climbing into his car. "But that didn't affect me in the least," he assured the judge. "It was the cigar I had afterward that made me dizzy."

"Twenty-five dollars," snapped the judge, "for driving while under the influence of a cigar."

A man in Columbia, South Carolina, was trying to explain to the judge how his accident came about: "Your Honor, last night I said to my wife, 'Let's go for a drive.' In ten minutes she was ready and we started across the river. Well, sir, do you know what? The car ran off the bridge and sank in the river, but a big dog dived in and rescued us. Then he went back up on the highway and barked for help . . . What are you grinning about, Your Honor? Don't you believe me?"

"Yep," said the judge, "all except that ridiculous part about your wife being ready in ten minutes."

Police apprehended a woman in Chisholm, Minnesota, when she was found behind the wheel of her car in the nude. The judge asked her to explain her lack of clothing. The woman said she was a "camel in

175

Morocco" and that all the palm trees lining the road proved it.

A teenage girl in Coatesville, Pennsylvania, was nabbed for driving down a highway in reverse. Her explanation? She explained to the judge how she'd run up too much mileage on the family car and just wanted to unwind some.

In Salem, Oregon, a woman was arrested for stopping her car in the middle of a busy intersection. She told the judge it was a case of emergency: "Baby's diaper needed changing."

A woman in Roanoke, Virginia, drove her car into one operated by a man and won a suspended sentence by explaining to the judge: "This was the first time I had driven alone, and my instructor said I was a perfect driver. But when I saw the other driver I got flustered."

"Why should he make you nervous?" asked the judge.

"The other driver, Your Honor, was my instructor."

A judge in Ellsworth, Maine, asked a driver: "How did you happen to hit this man?"

176

"I didn't hit him," the driver answered. "I stopped to let him go by, and I guess he was so surprised he fainted."

A judge in Lebanon, Tennessee, growled at the culprit before him: "I'm told that this is the fifth person you've knocked down with your car this year."

"That's not true, Your Honor!" shouted the man in righteous indignation. "One of them was the same person twice!"

A magistrate in Wichita, Kansas, was confronted again and again by a man arrested for every form of traffic violation—passing red lights, making improper turns, parking next to fire hydrants, driving while drunk, driving a car with faulty brakes, etc. After taking the offender's license away, the judge was shocked to see him once again: "I thought that I'd revoked your driving license."

"You did, Your Honor," the defendant admitted, "but this ticket is different—it's for jaywalking!"

The sheriff of Fitzgerald, Georgia, arrested one of the community's leading matrons for driving through a stop light. The woman insisted she had not seen it, claiming the light was newly installed behind a tree.

177

Nevertheless, the old southern judge found her guilty and fined her seven dollars or seven days. She refused to pay, accusing the whole administration of corruption and demanding that she be allowed to serve out her sentence in the local jail. The judge urged her to pay the seven dollars, go home, and forget the entire matter. But the southern lady was adamant, finally grabbing her jailer by the necktie and marching him toward the jailhouse. In jail she looked in horror at the suite she was to call home for the next seven days. In no uncertain terms she demanded that the bed be rid of bugs, a curtain provided, and a chair furnished.

"Send for the judge!" she cried. The judge arrived, listened patiently, then went into consultation with the jailer. A moment later he returned, flushed and triumphant.

"You win, ma'am," he announced gallantly. "The boys pooled their money and paid your fine. They just figure this jail is no place for a lady."

A Rugby, North Dakota, woman was caught driving with a plastic bag over her head. Booked for reckless driving, she won an acquittal by having the judge try the bag on and discover for himself that he could see through it.

178

Drivers' descriptions of their accidents as given in court vary extensively. Here are a few of the more oddball excuses told to the judge:

An elderly gentleman in Hartford, Wisconsin, offered this one: "I was on my way to the doctor with rear-end trouble when my universal joint gave way, causing me to have an accident."

Said a young lady in Elk City, Oklahoma: "The pedestrian had no idea which direction to go, so I ran over him."

Volunteered a fellow from Syracuse, New York, "I saw the slow-moving, sad-faced old gentleman as he bounced off the hood of my car."

Explained a woman in Casper, Wyoming, "The indirect cause of the accident was a little guy in a small car with a big mouth."

Then there was the fellow in Vicksburg, Mississippi, who said: "An invisible car came out of nowhere, struck my vehicle, and vanished."

179

A Woonsocket, Rhode Island, man was arrested for driving under the influence. He kept a straight face while telling the judge how he'd been mistakenly arrested for the same charge in the past. "Whenever I eat black-eyed peas and corn on the cob," he explained, "my breath smells as if I've been drinking."

18

Excuses! Excuses! Speeders and the Judge

A multitude of funny things can happen in the eternal duel between motorists and the police. Let's take a humorous peek at some of the most outlandish excuses used by drivers throughout the United States who got caught while exceeding the speed limit. Included are a variety of strange things these men and women have done when pulled over for breaking the law by speeding.

For example, a businessman was stopped on Highway 79 while on his way to work one morning in Pine Bluff, Arkansas. He quietly watched as a state trooper methodically wrote him a ticket for speeding. He later protested to the judge that this was this first speeding ticket. The judge handed down his decision with this reply: "Then, sir, we'll both have something to remember. This is the first fine I've ever given out." It was the young judge's first day on the job!

A man was caught speeding down Highway 70 while on his way home after a ball game in Marysville, California. The culprit tried this excuse out on the judge: "Your Honor, my wife was going to get pregnant that night, and I wanted to be there when she did."

A Florida highway patrolman stopped a fellow on Highway 24 outside of Gainesville for going over seventy miles an hour. Seems the guy was on his way home after playing a round of golf. The speeder told the judge, "My tires are bad, and I just wanted to get home before they give out."

A policeman in Bristol, Connecticut, pulled over a young fellow who was speeding on Highway 72. "As I approached the driver," explained the officer to the judge, "the man flipped open his wallet and spoke into it, saying, 'Kirk to *Enterprise*, Kirk to *Enterprise*, beam me out of here fast!' " The judge was so taken by the originality of this loony tune that the speeding culprit was let go with only a warning not to speed again.

It was the familiar scene of the police officer overhauling the young woman and her boyfriend out joyriding on Highway 332 just outside of Muncie, Indiana.

"Miss," said the judge, "you were doing better than sixty-five miles an hour."

"Oh," exclaimed the speeding driver, "isn't that wonderful for my first day of driving!"

In Pocatello, Idaho, two sisters were taken before the judge by a motorcycle policeman. Said the magistrate, "I see that according to this ticket, you were driving through a forty-mile zone at fifty miles an hour."

"Well, what of it?" said one of the two siblings. "The dealer who sold us the car said we could go as fast as we liked after the first thousand miles."

In Fairbanks, Alaska, a woman was speeding just outside of town on Highway 6 while on her way to a bowling match. She used her imagination and humored the court into an acquittal—by explaining that she'd just purchased a new hat and wanted to get to the game before it went out of style.

A police officer pulled a Dillon, Montana, speeder over on Highway 41. The culprit told the officer he didn't know he'd been speeding: "Seems I was preoccupied with killing a bee that had flown into my jacket, and my foot must have pushed the gas pedal down a little too much."

183

As evidence, the speeder produced a dead bee. "I asked the gentleman if I could see it a little closer," said the police officer to the judge. "The bee he showed me had dust on its wings. This bee had been dead for months, and he carried it in his pocket in case he ever got stopped.

"After I gave this man his ticket, he told me that his dead bee had always worked well in the past!"

A fellow in San Antonio was accused of going over the speed limit when rushing away from a busy intersection. The driver told the judge that he had to make a fast getaway. His wife was coming up San Pedro Avenue, and his girlfriend was snuggling up to him in the front seat!

A man was caught speeding on Highway 39 outside of Somerset, Kentucky. He tried to explain to the judge how he'd been distracted and hadn't watched his speedometer. According to this wayward speeder, his wife had been reading him an article on the dangers of going too fast.

A police officer stopped a speeder on Highway 64 near Hagerstown, Maryland, and pulled out his ticket book. "I clocked you at sixty-five, mister," he said to the speeder. Later, in court, the lady who was sitting

184

beside the driver cackled gleefully. "Just you put him in jail or give him a fine, Judge," she said. "Serves him right. He's a reckless, inconsiderate, dangerous driver."

"Your wife?" asked the judge. The driver glumly nodded his head. The magistrate smiled and said, "Case dismissed."

A man was charged with speeding down Highway 63 near Waterloo, Iowa. He later explained to the judge: "The sunshine, the clear road, and the additional stimulus of the car close behind me (not recognized as a police vehicle) undoubtedly gave added impetus to my psyche."

A nurse in Mobile, Alabama, was ticketed for speeding on her way to visit a sick friend. She tried her best to get the court not to give her a fine. Her excuse? She told the judge she had to drive fast in order to prevent amorous men on Government Boulevard from jumping into her convertible!

A mild-mannered young fellow in Hawthorne, Nevada, was stopped for speeding down Highway 95. Turns out he was also driving without a valid license. The speeder protested to the judge that he couldn't get one because of poor vision. His job? Attendant in a parking garage!

A woman in Haleiwa, Hawaii, was caught going sixty-five miles an hour in a forty-five-mile zone on Highway 83. The speeder later told the judge that she'd forgotten to take her birth control pill. And she had been merely rushing home to get one before it was too late. The judge, while acknowledging the originality of her excuse, fined her anyway!

A man was picked up for speeding on Highway 30 near Somerdale, New Jersey. He told the judge he'd been speeding only because he was late. And this was because of the farewell party given for his wife by a group of summer camp kids with speech impairments who had been taking speech lessons from her. Their appreciative comments had lasted much longer than expected!

A police officer stopped a speeder on Highway 7 just outside of Rutland, Vermont. Later, asked by the court why he was displaying the bumper stickers of two rival candidates for judge, he replied: "With my driving record, I can't afford to be wrong!"

At Haines City, Florida, a motorist charged with speeding blamed it all on his mother-in-law. He explained to the judge: "She had been staying with the family a week, and he was rushing to get her back to her own home."

A New York state trooper caught a fellow speeding down Highway 97 near Callicoon. The lawbreaker was riding in the center lane reserved for left turns. The violator's excuse? "Gee, Judge, I thought the center lane was put there for cars that wanted to go faster."

A fellow was stopped for going seventy-two miles an hour on Highway 6 just before entering Frances, Washington. The driver pointed out to the judge: "I couldn't keep my eyes on the speedometer, Your Honor, because I was too busy pouring a cup of coffee."

Two truckers in Peoria, Illinois, shelled out $35 apiece on speeding tickets. The men then asked the judge to fine the arresting officer $25 for littering Highway 68 with the two carbons from his ticket book. He did!

But sometimes the law has the last laugh. A fellow in Tucumcari, New Mexico, grudgingly paid his fine for speeding down Highway 209. The judge then ordered the fellow to hand over an extra $50 because he had made his check out to the "Police Gestapo."

A speeding clergyman in Shreveport, Louisiana, was on his way to church. He was stopped by the police on Highway 71 and charged with speeding. The minister was going seventy-three miles an hour. He casually explained to the judge, "You have to travel fast these days in order to save souls." The judge said he would not levy a fine—if the clergyman would preach one sermon every twelve months on driving safety.

A woman in Wilmington, Delaware, testified that she wasn't speeding when pulled over on Highway 52. The woman explained to the judge, "I don't have to watch the speedometer. I can just feel how fast my car is going."

"And I just feel you can't," replied the judge, banging his gavel and fining her $45.

A bakery owner in Columbia, Missouri, had a strange excuse for speeding down Highway 63! Seems he had taken a break on the way home after work to play softball. The game lasted longer than expected, and the fellow found he had to make up some time. He told the judge he was going fast "so the whipped cream on my cupcakes wouldn't turn sour."

"Judge, so help me, I wasn't going sixty-three miles an hour like the officer says. I wasn't going fifty-three miles an hour. I wasn't even . . ." pleaded the worried fellow who had been picked up for speeding on Highway 117 near Goldsboro, North Carolina, while rushing home in his pickup truck.

"Stop!" said the judge. "We'd better close this case before you start backing up and hurt somebody. Thirty dollars."

A fellow was pulled over on Highway 55 just before entering Cadillac, Michigan. The officer tried to administer a breathalizer test. The speeder wouldn't cooperate. "That's the same as refusing," the officer later testified in court. But the speeder vehemently denied this: "I couldn't blow into the machine because I've got false teeth, and when I blow, it blows them out." The case was dismissed.

The highway patrol was led on a frenzied chase down Highway 522 just outside of Culpeper, Virginia. The speeder was eventually pulled over. The driver explained to the judge: "I was in a hurry to get to a garage in order to have my brakes checked."

She was an innocent-appearing woman as she sat on the witness stand in Fort Collins, Colorado, explaining how it was all wrong that she'd been given a ticket for speeding. Even the gray-maned judge took a fatherly interest in her and decided to be lenient.

"Now, my dear," he said, "I'm inclined to believe you, but I want to make sure. You know what happens to people who tell lies in court, don't you?"

"Yes, Your Honor. My lawyer told me about it."

"What did he tell you would happen if you told a lie?"

"Well, he said we *might* win the case."

Index